EXPECTING Joy

EXPECTING Joy

by Mary Lou Graham
and
Marianne Kelso

LEGACY PRESS
A Division of Rainbow Publishers

To our mothers

Mary (Rusty) Peters

for lighting up our home with laughter. — MLG

and

Betty M. Rossmiller

for birthing and courageously raising eleven children. — MK

EXPECTING JOY
©2007 by Legacy Press, seventh printing
ISBN 10: 1-885358-62-8
ISBN 13: 978-1-885358-62-2
Legacy reorder# LP46841
Christian living/practical life/women

Legacy Press
P.O. Box 70130
Richmond, VA 23255

Unless otherwise noted, Scriptures are from the *Holy Bible: New International Version* (North American Edition), copyright ©1973, 1978, 1984 by the International Bible Society. Used by permission of Zondervan Bible Publishers.

Scripture quotations marked NASB are taken from the NEW AMERICAN STANDARD BIBLE ®, Copyright © 1960, 1962, 1963, 1968, 1971, 1972, 1973, 1975, 1977, 1995 by The Lockman Foundation. Used by permission.

Printed in the United States of America

Table of Contents

Preface

There are often seasons in our lives when we don't understand the timing of the Lord, but we trust His hand upon us. When we agreed to write this book, it was with some hesitation because of the difficulty in carving out time in our schedules. We both wanted to keep the Lord, our husbands and our children as our priorities. We prayed, discussed it with our husbands, and came up with schedules that we thought would work for our families.

A couple of weeks into writing, Mary Lou found out she was pregnant. She and her husband, Rich, were excited but also a little overwhelmed. After nine years of marriage, they already had an eight-year-old, a five-year-old and a toddler. Each of Mary Lou's pregnancies had gotten more physically challenging, and they wondered how she would be able to take care of the children daily, much less write a book.

Marianne and her husband, Tim, sensed that their family was incomplete. For eight years they had been praying and waiting on God for another child. Just one month after agreeing to write this book, Marianne discovered she was pregnant. She and Tim were thrilled, and so were their eleven-year-old and nine-year-old children. Though they were amazed at God's faithfulness, they knew it would be quite a challenge to write a book during the early stages of pregnancy.

It soon became evident, though, that God's timing was perfect. Besides blessing us with children, He was blessing this book by giving us "fresh manna"! This book was not written from hours of quiet study in a library filled with theology books. It was written in the trenches of battle. In the midst of nausea. In the middle of migraines. In the joy of anticipation. We wrote this book as we traveled the gamut of emotions that accompany pregnancy. This is not a textbook of the way things should be. Instead this is a testimony to the mercy and grace of the Lord toward the women He has chosen to bear His children.

Isaiah 40:11 says that the Lord "tends his flock like a shepherd: He gathers the lambs in his arms and carries them close to his heart; *he gently leads those that have young*" (emphasis added). You became a mother in your heart the day you found out you were pregnant. You began to view life differently, make changes for the health of your baby, and prepare for your baby's arrival. You are a mother and God is preparing you to receive this precious gift from Him.

The season of pregnancy is an excellent time to nurture the child within you, and to nurture the fruits of the Spirit listed in Galatians 5:22 — love, self-control, peace, goodness, kindness, faithfulness, gentleness, patience and joy. We have arranged these nine fruits to correspond to the nine months of pregnancy. Therefore, this book can be read consecutively from the beginning of pregnancy to the end, or you can turn to a specific topic when you need encouragement in that area.

Many books on the market today make the reader feel good – temporarily. We believe that the power of Scripture changes lives forever. Each devotional is built upon Bible verses and true examples of how God cares for us through pregnancy. Journal pages with questions are included for each day's readings so that your insights and memories can be recorded for yourself, your child and generations to come.

It is our prayer that this book will cause you to reflect fondly on the baby growing within you, challenge you spiritually and encourage your relationship with the Lord.

Mary Lou Graham
&
Marianne Kelso

Love

Sow for yourselves righteousness, reap the fruit of unfailing love, and break up your unplowed ground; for it is time to seek the Lord, until he comes and showers righteousness on you.

Hosea 10:12

The Shepherd

The Lord is near to all who call on him,
to all who call on him in truth.
Psalm 145:18

It's 3:36 a.m.! Why am I still awake? I'm pregnant. I'm tired. I need rest. But I can't get comfortable. My back aches. My legs ache. My brain aches from thinking so much. I just want to sleep!

My only comfort is that though my family is asleep, and the house is dark and quiet, I am not alone. What an amazing thought! It doesn't matter what time it is, or where we are. When we call out to the Lord, He is there. "He will not let your foot slip — he who watches over you will not slumber" (Psalm 121:3). The Lord does not sleep. He is always watching over us. And if those times in the middle of the night are filled with crying, the Bible says that He keeps our tears in a bottle (Psalm 56:8 NASB). Oh, the love that He has for us! We are truly the apple of His eye (Psalm 17:8).

The Bible paints a beautiful portrait of the Lord's love. He is described as a shepherd watching over us, His sheep. Isaiah 40:11 says, "He tends his flock like a shepherd: He gathers the lambs in his arms and carries them close to his heart; he gently leads those that have young."

Ladies, we need that help and guidance. But what happens when we leave the safety of the green pastures? What happens when we stray onto the rocky paths of the world and lose sight of our Shepherd? The Bible says the shepherd will go after the lost sheep until he finds it. "And when he finds it, he joyfully puts it on his shoulders and goes home. Then he calls his friends and neighbors together and says, 'Rejoice with me; I have found my lost sheep'" (Luke 15:5-6).

Are you a lost sheep? When you look about you now, can you see the Shepherd? Do you have the joy and peace of daily following and trusting the Good Shepherd? Or have you walked so far into the rocks and weeds that you don't think you can find your way back to the green pastures? You sought after what you thought was a lovely red flower blooming just over that boulder, but it turned out to be a piece of discarded trash, and now you are miles from the flock.

Look up. Take your eyes off of the slippery rocks beneath your feet and look up on the horizon. It is the Shepherd, calling out for you. Calling you by name (John 10:3). He has come in search of you. Answer Him. Answer Him today. "My sheep listen to my voice; I know them, and they follow me. I give them eternal life, and they shall never perish; no one can snatch them out of my hand" (John 10:27-28).

Or maybe all you have ever known is a life surrounded by the jagged cliffs and prickly thorns of sin. Maybe you have never known the love of the Shepherd and the peace of living in His pasture. No matter what pit of sin you are in, the Shepherd can pull you out. Luke 13:3 says that the Lord does not want anyone to perish, but wants everyone to come to repentance.

And that is the key: repentance. "If we confess our sins, he is faithful and just and will forgive us our sins and purify us from all unrighteousness" (1 John 1:9). Confess your sin to the Lord today. Call on Him and confess your need for His salvation. He will lift you up and set you in the green pastures of His love.

–MLG

Prayer

Lord, I thank You for Your love. I thank You that You call out to me when I am lost. I thank You that when I call out to You, You are near no matter where I am. Help me to respond to Your love. Amen.

For further study ~ John 10:1-30

My Shepherd

If I have never been in the green pastures of the Shepherd's love, I cry out to the Lord today (date:_____):

Lord, I am a sinner. Please forgive my sins and bring me into Your flock. I want to hear Your voice and follow You. I give my life to You, and look forward to daily walking with You and spending eternity in heaven with You.

If I have strayed from the green pastures of the Shepherd's love, I cry out to the Lord today (date:_____).

Lord, please forgive me for turning away from You and pursuing my own sinful desires. What I thought was a little step on the ground of compromise has now led me into treacherous territory. I hear You calling my name and I am calling out to You. Please help me and carry me home on Your shoulders.

If I am firmly and safely in the green pastures of the Shepherd's love, I commit today to faithfully pray for those people who do not know the joy of Your love (date:_7-17-08_____).

*Then we your people, the sheep of your pasture,
will praise you forever; from generation to
generation we will recount your praise.
~ Psalm 79:13*

God's Household

Consequently, you are no longer foreigners and aliens, but fellow citizens with God's people and members of God's household.
Ephesians 2:19

"No, honey, Mommy can't play right now. I'm still eating. No, you can't play in Mommy's food. Where are you going? The bathroom? No, no. Don't play with the toilet. Just wait a minute. I'm almost done eating."

Dinner time was becoming a nightmare. My toddler always finished first, and I'd take her out of the highchair to let her play in her room. Well, that was the theory, but it never happened that way. I was at a loss until a friend from church had a great idea: teach my toddler to sit in the highchair and look at books until everyone was done eating. It would make our meals at home more peaceful and certainly make our time at restaurants more enjoyable.

Why didn't I think of that? I don't know, but I'm sure glad my friend felt the freedom to offer advice. In fact, this is only one of countless times when I've been glad to have counsel from friends.

Parenting can be challenging and confusing. Sometimes, the little decisions can be more overwhelming than the big ones. We will need help raising our children. We will need help from our family — the household of God.

1 Timothy 3:15 defines God's household as "the church of the living God." And in this household, the members have certain responsibilities. Galatians 6:10 says we are to "do good to all people, especially to those who belong to the family of believers." When I come home from the hospital in a couple of months with a new baby, I'll need some of that "good." I'll need my family of believers to bring me meals and give me calls to make sure I'm adjusting all right and actually finding time to at least brush my teeth each day.

The members of our church family are also called to "correct, rebuke and encourage — with great patience and careful instruction" (2 Timothy 4:2). Amen! That is exactly what I'll need. I know I'll have blind spots as I raise this child. I need godly people who love me enough to point out my mistakes, so I don't look back ten years later with regret and say, "I didn't know."

I need people around me who are also committed to raising children who love and obey the Lord. I need the encouragement of knowing I'm not alone. I need wise Christians to instruct me and share with me what they've learned. I need my child to grow up with friends who worship God, read the Bible, and say no to the trappings of the world. I need the household of God! And you need the household of God.

Now is an excellent time to evaluate your involvement in the church. Are you part of a church that teaches the Word of God? Are you part of a church where the members treat each other like family, sharing both the good times and the bad? Have you opened yourself up to friends in your church so that they have the freedom to "correct, rebuke, and encourage" you?

It is a harsh world out there, and God has created us to need each other. This becomes even more apparent as we begin the daunting task of raising children. Let's make whatever changes are needed now, so that when our babies enter this world, they will have a family of believers waiting to welcome them.

–MLG

Prayer

I thank You, Father, for creating the church and giving us a family committed to You. I know that in many ways, You express Your love to me through my brothers and sisters in Christ. Thank You for making me a part of Your household. Amen.

For further study ~ Acts 2:42-47

My Family of Believers

Do I view the members of my church as part of my family?

Some - I guess mostly my close
friends that go to Fellowship

How does this affect the way I interact with them?

I'm more comfortable around them

How does this view affect the way I receive their help?

I'm not very good at accepting help, but
I know I'll need it with the baby.

Which Christian friends have I asked to "correct, rebuke and encourage me?"

Jerra, Cristen, Kourtney

Whom should I ask?

Barbara, Kelsy?

Instead, speaking the truth in love,
we will in all things grow up into him
who is the Head, that is, Christ.
~ Ephesians 4:15

Someone to Pray for Us

*Who is he that condemns? Christ Jesus, who died —
more than that, who was raised to life — is at the right
hand of God and is also interceding for us.*
Romans 8:34

I've read books and magazines, and even watched videos, about pregnancy, birth, and caring for a newborn. I've studied medical books about how to handle childhood sicknesses and emergencies. I've devoured books on parenting and I've attended parenting seminars. I have absorbed all of the knowledge I can and am now ready to raise my child.

Wrong! There is one thing we can be sure of as parents: the unexpected will happen. We will be going about our normal life when suddenly it hits. A suspicious lump on the neck. Unidentifiable mucus running out of the ear. A seizure in the middle of the night. Sometimes split-second decisions are required. How will we know what to do?

Medical surprises aren't all that we'll face. There will also be emotional and spiritual ones. A child who is visiting says your child hit him. Your child denies it. Your child comes home crying because someone made fun of her father. A close friend dies, and your child wants to know if he is in heaven. How will we know what to do?

It would help if we knew what was going to happen tomorrow. Then we would have time to pray specifically and be prepared.

We don't know what tomorrow holds, but there is someone who does. Colossians 2:3 says that in Christ are hidden "all the treasures of wisdom and knowledge." Jesus Christ knows everything and has the wisdom for every situation. But how does that help us?

After Jesus was crucified, He rose from the grave three days later and spoke to many on earth. Then the Bible says He was taken up into heaven and seated at the right hand of God (Mark 16:19). Is He just sitting there now on His throne, watching us and hoping everything turns out all right? No, He is interceding for us! The Son of God, who knows everything that has happened and will happen, is our advocate. That is amazing love!

It is always comforting to know that someone is praying for us. How much more so to know the Son of God is interceding for us.

–MLG

Prayer

Lord, I want to be responsible and learn as much as I can about children, but I know I can't be prepared for everything. I am so glad that I have You to lean on. It is comforting to know that You are my advocate, even before I know what will happen. Thank You for this wonderful expression of love. Amen.

For further study ~ Psalm 57

Jesus Christ Is My Advocate

What can I do to remember that Christ is interceding for me?

When I get panicked, I can remember.

I can get up in the morning + say it out loud whether I'm worried or not

Am I thankful that Christ is interceding for me? How should that affect my attitude toward the future?

Very thankful — I shouldn't panic or worry

In what ways has the Lord showed His love toward me?

Forgiveness + mercy

Ben   Family

Baby   Friends

LIFE

For I am convinced that neither death
nor life, neither angels nor demons, neither the
present nor the future, nor any powers, neither
height nor depth, nor anything else in all creation,
will be able to separate us from the love of
God that is in Christ Jesus our Lord.
~ Romans 8:38-39

The Ninth Child

Like arrows in the hands of a warrior are sons born in one's youth. Blessed is the man whose quiver is full of them.
Psalm 127:4-5

My father was never ashamed to say he had eleven children. He knew the blessing of God was upon him because of all of his children. I am very grateful that my parents did not limit the size of their family and that they chose to give me life. I love being the ninth child of eleven! Whenever my family gathers, it is a party. My baby will be the thirtieth grandchild for my parents.

"Children's children are a crown to the aged, and parents are the pride of their children" (Proverbs 17:6).

Whether we got pregnant while using three forms of birth control or whether we used fertility drugs to conceive, the central issue is the same: we carry a blessing from God within us. Birth control is a personal conviction between God, your husband and you. This is not about birth control, it is about our attitude toward the blessings that we carry within us now.

These babies are going to make our families larger. Our lives are about to expand. If we're concerned about the size of our family, we need to take a fresh look at God's perspective. Children are a reward and a heritage from God (Psalm 127:3). No child is a mistake in the eyes of God.

Not every day is a picnic in the park when you have many children. It is downright difficult. But life is a challenge no matter what circumstances we face. Hasn't God promised to be there for us in our weaknesses? 2 Corinthians 12:9 encourages us, "'My grace is sufficient for you, for my power is made perfect in weakness.' Therefore I will boast all the more gladly about my weaknesses, so that Christ's power may rest on me."

Our children will test us in our weaknesses, but God is faithful to make us stronger in those areas. Our babies are a blessing to us, a means of sanctification, a means to make us stronger in Christ as we lean not to our own understanding but trust completely in God's sufficient grace (Proverbs 3:5).

–MK

Prayer

Thank You, Father, for the number of children You have given me. You chose to give me life. Now I have the special privilege of carrying this new life You have placed within me. I am grateful for the heritage this child brings. I ask for Your grace to manage this blessing for Your glory. Amen.

For further study ~ Psalm 128

My Reward

This is a rewarding time with my family that I remember from childhood: _____

_____

_____

_____

_____

This is my view on the size of my family. Does it line up with God's Word?

_____

_____

_____

How has God already used this baby to make me stronger in my weaknesses? _____

_____

_____

_____

_____

Her children arise and call her blessed;
her husband also, and he praises her.
~ Proverbs 31:28

Remain in Me

*If you remain in me and my words remain in you,
ask whatever you wish, and it will be given you.*
John 15:7

This Bible verse was sent to me from a friend who knew how much I wanted to be pregnant. It was neatly written on a piece of paper. Enclosed with it was a comforting letter. This friend had also tried for many years to get pregnant. Three children later, she had not forgotten the agony of waiting on God for something you want so desperately — something that God says is good. Her note reminded me to press into God in my time of need.

I took that little piece of paper and stuck it on my refrigerator. Every day I read it and reread it. When I did finally get pregnant, I knew my baby was an answer to prayer.

At that time, I was not walking with God as I am now. My only time with Him was when I stood before my refrigerator reading that verse. I attended church, but my heart was not in it. My heart was focused on becoming pregnant. Yet, reading this verse day after day, month after month, drew me to God and I began to allow His Words to remain in me. I was learning the benefits of biblical meditation. Soon I made Jesus Lord of my life. I saw how God had been graciously calling me, giving me the desires of my heart and loving me before I was capable of knowing His true love.

I began my relationship with the Lord by allowing His words to remain in me. But John 15:7 says that I am also to remain in Him. How do I do that?

Some of the ways we can remain in the Lord are by meditating on His Word, praying, fasting, worshipping, and studying the Bible and applying it to our lives. John 15:8 goes on to explain the benefits: "This is to my Father's glory, that you bear much fruit, showing yourselves to be my disciples." We can see here that bearing fruit is the result of remaining in the Lord.

Pregnancy is a time of preparation. God is preparing our babies to live outside our wombs, while we are preparing our homes to receive them. Yet have we considered that when our babies come, we won't have as much time to read God's Word? Now is the time to also prepare our hearts.

Life is busy. We can get caught up in what demands to be done and let God slip by as we are distracted by the urgent and overlooking what is important. Does this bear fruit for the Lord? Come, let us remain in God, making time to be with Him and showing ourselves to be His disciples.

–MK

Prayer

Father, show me how to spend quiet time with You to prepare me for the birth of my baby. Teach me to meditate on Your Word and show me the power of biblical meditation in my life. Help me to remain in You and to let Your words remain in me because my wish is to draw nearer to You. Amen.

For further study ~ John 15:1-17

How Can I Remain in Jesus?

What is my greatest wish right now? Is it a wish that would be to my Father's glory?

_____

_____

_____

_____

This Scripture has remained in me and has been a great comfort in difficult times: _____

_____

_____

_____

These are the preparations that I need to make in my heart for the birth of my baby: _____

_____

_____

_____

_____

All that belongs to the Father is mine.
That is why I said the Spirit will take from
what is mine and make it known to you.
~ John 16:15

I Passed the Test

Blessed is the man who perseveres under trial,
because when he has stood the test, he will receive the crown
of life that God has promised to those who love him.
James 1:12

My hands were shaking as I ripped open the pregnancy test. I was five days late. Could I really be pregnant? Was I starting an early menopause? It had been seven years since I was pregnant — ten since I carried to full-term. I had gotten my hopes up so many times that I tried not to think anything at all.

When two lines showed up on the pregnancy test, I couldn't believe it. I was pregnant! I said it over and over again in my mind, trying to convince myself that it was true.

Eight years ago I believed God told me that I would have a son. We began trying to get pregnant. Six months later I conceived, but the pregnancy ended in miscarriage. Years of dashed hopes followed. Eventually, I faced the fact that just because I believed God told me I would have a son did not mean it had to be true. If that was God's promise, then I would have a son someday. If not, and I misunderstood God, then He was still faithful and worthy to be served and praised. "Consider it pure joy, my brothers, whenever you face trials of many kinds, because you know that the testing of your faith develops perseverance. Perseverance must finish its work so that you may be mature and complete, not lacking anything" (James 1:2-4).

Not getting pregnant was a trial I faced every month. Yet, God gave me the ability to persevere year after year and not lose hope. On several occasions I doubted God. But He was gentle and kind and loved me through the doubts so I never lost my faith. When I saw God fulfill other promises, it encouraged me and built my faith.

When our faith wavers because of circumstances and unbelief, we need to remember that God is faithful. He is bigger than any trial. God can create a path that wasn't there a minute ago. Faith requires perseverance, and perseverance refines us into mature and complete Christians. When we have finished our life here on earth, God promises our perseverance will be rewarded with the crown of life (James 1:12).

Faith also requires hope: "Now faith is being sure of what we hope for and certain of what we do not see" (Hebrews 11:1). Whether we see that crown or not, we know what God has promised. Our job is to persevere in God's love and faithfulness until we see His promise fulfilled.

–MK

Prayer

Father, thank You for every promise You have fulfilled. Show me where I have passed the test so my faith may be built up and strengthened to persevere through to the promises not yet fulfilled. Amen.

For further study ~ 1 Peter 1:3-9

I Passed the Test

I persevered through this trial to see God's faithfulness revealed to me:

_____

_____

_____

_____

This is a trial I am persevering through right now: _____

_____

_____

_____

_____

This is my story of how I found out I was pregnant and my response to the news: _____

_____

_____

_____

_____

Test me, O Lord, and try me, examine my heart and my mind; for your love is ever before me, and I walk continually in your truth.
~ Psalm 26:2-3

God Opens the Womb

*Then God remembered Rachel;
listened to her and opened her womb.*
Genesis 30:22

took eighteen months for me to get pregnant the first time; the second time it happened after the first try; and then we tried eight years for the third child. Why is it so easy sometimes? At other times it can be so hard!

In this society we are led to believe that we can choose when we want to have children: "I want to get pregnant in the fall, so I'm going off the pill in June." Or we believe we will get pregnant if we don't use birth control one time. Certainly that happens, but when the miracle of conception takes place, the hand of God is there from the beginning (Psalm 139:13). Birth control is not controlling our fertility. Women get pregnant while using birth control all of the time. No birth control is 100 percent guaranteed. However, there are many women who have a difficult time getting pregnant. They spend thousands of dollars to find out why. There are cases that cannot be explained by modern technology.

Genesis 29:31 says, "When the Lord saw that Leah was not loved, he opened her womb, but Rachel was barren." The Bible also says that the Lord closed Hannah's womb (1 Samuel 1:5). It is the Lord who opens and closes wombs — then and now.

We rejoice that God has chosen to open our wombs. He has a plan for us and our babies. So whether this child we carry was conceived after much prayer, or whether this conception was a complete surprise, God knew the plans He had for these precious lives before time began (Jeremiah 1:5).

–MK

Prayer

God, thank You for opening my womb with Your sovereign hand. Thank You for choosing to give my baby life at this time. Help me to remember that You are bigger than my actions and that You know what is best for me and for my baby. Amen.

For further study ~ Genesis 29:31–30:24

God Opened My Womb

What was my response when I found out I was pregnant? Did I see it as God opening my womb? _____

_____

_____

_____

_____

_____

_____

In what way have I seen the hand of God in the conception of my baby?

_____

_____

_____

_____

How has waiting for this pregnancy, or being surprised by it, affected my walk with God? _____

_____

_____

_____

He settles the barren woman in her home as a happy mother of children. Praise the Lord.
~ Psalm 113:9

Beauty

For the Lord takes pleasure in His people;
He will beautify the afflicted ones with salvation.
Psalm 149:4 NASB

I quickly told everyone I met at my friend's wedding that I was pregnant. Yes, I was excited about having a baby, but I must admit that was not my primary motive. What was underlying my simple announcement was a deeper, stronger desire to declare: I'm not out of shape! I'm pregnant!

For I was at that in-between stage. Not big enough to look pregnant, just misshapen enough to look like I was in desperate need of a few aerobic classes.

It was in this condition that I met the woman in black. The toned, flat-bellied woman in black. She slinked up to me with her fiancé and I immediately informed them of my pregnancy. My husband enthusiastically joined in and commented that they too may one day be expecting a baby of their own. The sleek woman in black looked at my lumpy body and coolly replied, "Oh, I don't think I could ever let that happen to my body."

"That"? It was the disgust in the woman's voice that jolted me from my self-absorbed and worldly perspective. What was I thinking? It was a blessing "that" was happening to my body. It was a gift from God causing "that" to happen to my body. "That" was a beautiful thing happening to my body.

And "that" was the problem. My definition of beauty had been tainted by the world. We are Christian women. According to Colossians 2:8, we are not to fall prey to the empty philosophies of the world. We are not to be conformed to the image of some supermodel; we are to be conformed to the image of Christ (Romans 8:29).

The world's idea of beauty changes over time. Just looking at artwork from the renaissance period, for example, shows how the definition of beauty has changed. We do not want to spend our time and money trying to reach an arbitrary standard of beauty defined by a group of strangers whose lives are probably ungodly. Proverbs 23:17 says, "Do not let your heart envy sinners, but always be zealous for the fear of the Lord." According to Psalm 27:6, it is the Lord who lifts our head up high, not pride in our appearance.

True beauty is found in the Lord, and serving Him. Psalm 50:2 says that God is "perfect in beauty." And Romans 10:15 says, "How beautiful are the feet of those who bring good news!" May we reevaluate our priorities and join with the psalmist in crying out with his one request: "that I may dwell in the house of the Lord all the days of my life, to gaze upon the beauty of the Lord and to seek him in his temple" (Psalm 27:4).

–MLG

Prayer

Lord, I want to look my best and take care of the body You have given me. But I do not want it to be my passion. I do not want my appearance to absorb time and money that could be more wisely spent in other ways. I want to have the confidence that You created me and formed me. I am beautiful because I am Your daughter. Amen.

For further study ~ Isaiah 3:16-18

The Beauty in Me

Where do I find my definition of beauty? From television? Movies?
Magazines? _____

_____

_____

Whom have I set as my role model? A glamorous figure from
Hollywood? Or even myself from younger years? Is this image I am
conforming to a worthy one or a worldly one? _____

_____

_____

_____

Have I been looking to someone on earth to build my confidence and
lift my head? That's a tough burden to put on anyone. How can I
change my lifestyle to spend more time with my Father, the one who
created me, and valued me enough to save me? _____

_____

_____

_____

*Do not conform any longer to
the pattern of this world, but be transformed
by the renewing of your mind. Then you
will be able to test and approve what God's
will is — his good, pleasing and perfect will.
~ Romans 12:2*

Self-Control

Now for this very reason also, applying all diligence, in your faith supply moral excellence, and in your moral excellence, knowledge, and in your knowledge, self-control, and in your self-control, perseverance, and in your perseverance, godliness, and in your godliness, brotherly kindness, and in your brotherly kindness, love. For if these qualities are yours and are increasing, they render you neither useless nor unfruitful in the true knowledge of our Lord Jesus Christ.

2 Peter 1:5-8 NASB

A Priceless Treasure

But if we have food and clothing, we will be content with that.
1 Timothy 6:8

I'm taking a "just in case" pregnancy test. I'm scheduled for oral surgery tomorrow, and I'll need a lot of pain-killers. My conscience will feel much better knowing for certain that there is no unexpected little life inside me.

I'd rather wait to have the surgery, but my husband will be losing his job soon, and I need to have it completed while we still have insurance. So, I guess we'll load up our five-person family into our only car — a five-seater — and head to the doctor's office tomorrow.

All right, five minutes have passed. I'll just throw the test away and…what's this? It's positive? I'm pregnant? Now? What timing! We'll need a job, a van, a bed…

My mind was a jumble throughout the day as I was reminded of more and more things we would need for a new baby. Finally that evening, I settled down and turned on a worship music tape. As the melody filled the room, and eventually my mind, I began to think clearly for the first time that day. I should have one and only one response to the news I received today: I should fall on my knees and worship the Lord for giving me a child.

"And my God will meet all your needs according to his glorious riches in Christ Jesus" (Philippians 4:19). Our children are gifts from God and we can depend on Him to provide for their needs. What may be required on our part, though, is a change of perspective.

The truth is, each one of these gifts comes with a price tag. Not just the cost of our time, but there is also a very real financial cost. Even once we get past the medical bills of pregnancy and birth, there is the daily expense of supporting a child. And this cost often translates into a lifestyle modification and sacrifice of material possessions.

Let's look at that term "sacrifice." It implies that something has been given up, and a standard has not been reached. When we gauge our financial condition, whose standard are we using? For most of us, having a child will not require us to sacrifice food or the clothing off our backs. We may have to forgo going out to eat or having designer clothes, but is that a true sacrifice?

It's very easy to let the world dictate our expected standard of living. Marketers scream out at us through commercials and advertisements, trying to convince us that we cannot survive without their product. But do these promoters have our best interests in mind? It is not the products themselves that are wrong, it is our response that is wrong if we embrace the philosophy of the world that says if it's better than what you have, buy it!

And how do material "blessings" compare to the blessings of children? Jesus says in Matthew 6:19, "Do not store up for yourselves treasures on earth, where moth and rust destroy, and where thieves break in and steal." In contrast, Psalm 127:3 says, "Sons are a heritage from the Lord, children a reward from him." You may have to say no to many things you want because of your child. But you are saying yes to a little head resting contentedly on your shoulder as you rock in the quiet of the night. Yes to a tiny hand grasping your finger. Yes to chubby arms reaching out for a hug. And yes to the lifetime joy of being called Mommy.

Do not look with regret at the things you will be giving up. Instead, set your heart on the true wealth that awaits you — a treasure chest of priceless moments with your child. The joy of loving and being loved is more valuable than material possessions that rust, decay and become useless.

–MLG

Prayer

Lord, I do not want to elevate temporal belongings above the lifetime gift of a child. Keep far from me the lies and falsehoods of the world that say I must have a certain standard of living. Please help me as I make the necessary lifestyle changes to accommodate my new baby, for I know that children are an awesome investment with tremendous rewards. Amen.

For further study ~ 1 Timothy 6:3-21

My Priceless Treasure

Have I allowed financial concerns to interfere with the joy of having a child? If so, here is my prayer of repentance: _____

_____

_____

_____

_____

What material things have I come to expect in my life? Are these things I truly need, or are they just things I want? _____

_____

_____

When I look back thirty years from now, what will I treasure? Am I investing in those things today?

_____

_____

Whoever welcomes one of these little children in my name welcomes me; and whoever welcomes me does not welcome me but the one who sent me.
~ Mark 9:37

Heartbeat of Life

Jesus answered, "It is written: 'Man does not live on bread alone, but on every word that comes from the mouth of God.'"
Matthew 4:4

As I lay on the examining table hearing the swoosh-swoosh of my baby's heartbeat, tears sprang from my eyes. Were they tears of joy? Yes, but they were mixed with tears of guilt. There was a life growing in me! It was at this moment that I realized the life I carried depended on what I ate, and a lot of what I had been eating was junk food. My baby needed healthy food to grow strong!

We need to eat the right things to nourish our baby's health. Instead of stopping for fast food, we need to plan ahead by bringing a healthy snack. When we are tempted to eat unhealthy food, the Holy Spirit is there, ready to help us reach for fruit — the fruit of self-control.

Let that digest a moment and consider that what we take in spiritually also affects our babies. How do we feed ourselves with God's Word? Here, too, we are given a choice. We can make it a fast food stop in the rush of our busy lives or we can plan ahead for a healthy grazing in the food God has given us for spiritual strength: the Bible. The fruit of self-control can be exercised as we plan our day. Because Jesus is Lord of our lives, we need to give Him quality time in our busy schedules. We can ask God to show us how and when we can make time for His Word each day.

In John 4:34 Jesus said, "My food is to do the will of him who sent me and to finish his work." God's will for us at this time is to nurture what He has given us — our own lives as well as our children's lives. To nurture our children we must first nurture ourselves physically and spiritually.

Leading these little ones to Christ begins now. Let's be sure that what we are feeding our children is nourishing their souls. Someday we may have the joy of seeing the fruit of the Spirit manifest in their lives.

–MK

Prayer

Father, I cry out to You in my lack of self-control. In my weakness I pray to You for strength to eat healthy meals and snacks that will nurture the growth of my baby. More importantly, help me choose to graze in Your Word for my own spiritual growth and that of my baby. Change me into the image of Your Son, Jesus, as I digest Your Word. Let my life bring glory to Your name as I lead my little one to You! Amen.

For further study ~ Isaiah 55

What Does My Heart Beat For?

This is everything I remember eating in the last twenty-four hours. Is my baby getting a healthy diet?

_____

_____

_____

_____

How have I spent time with God in the last twenty-four hours?

_____

_____

_____

Is this spiritual diet healthy enough to support two lives? Where do I need to change? _____

_____

_____

*So do not worry, saying,
"What shall we eat?" or "What shall we drink?"
or "What shall we wear?" For the pagans run
after all these things, and your heavenly Father
knows that you need them. But seek first his
kingdom and his righteousness, and all these
things will be given to you as well.
~ Matthew 6:31-33*

The Day Will Come

For you know very well that the day of the Lord will come like a thief in the night. While people are saying, "Peace and safety," destruction will come on them suddenly, as labor pains on a pregnant woman, and they will not escape.
1 Thessalonians 5:2-3

I was discouraged on the drive back from my obstetrician's office. I wanted to go into labor naturally, but I was already ten days late. This was getting ridiculous and I was getting huge. I had reluctantly agreed to be induced the next day.

Suddenly, a contraction gripped my womb, causing me to grip the door handle. This was no Braxton-Hicks contraction. This was the real thing.

That's one of the great things about pregnancy. No matter what else is going on, you can know this for sure: one way or another, that baby will come out!

The same is true for the second coming of the Lord. No matter what else is going on, we can know this for sure: Jesus Christ will return. Just as sure as He came the first time, He's coming again. The question is: are we ready?

Over the years, people have had strange responses to the second coming of Christ. Some have tried to predict the day. Some have sold all their belongings and quit their jobs to wait for the return of Christ, only to have to get new jobs and buy new things. The Bible is clear, though, that "no one knows about that day or hour, not even the angels in heaven, nor the Son, but only the Father" (Mark 13:32).

What does the Bible say our response should be? "So then, let us not be like others, who are asleep, but let us be alert and self-controlled" (1 Thessalonians 5:6). We are not to live our days in a spiritual slumber, lazy and apathetic about the choices we make. No, we are to be alert, waiting for the return of the Lord, and self-controlled, making wise decisions.

God could tell us when Christ will return. Instead, we are given the command to "live holy and godly lives as you look forward to the day of God and speed its coming" (2 Peter 3:11-12). Since we don't know the exact time of His return, we are to live every day as if He might come today.

Are we ready? If Jesus is Lord of our lives, then we have the assurance that we will be taken up into heaven. But what about the moment He arrives? What will He find us doing? "When the Son of Man comes, will he find faith on the earth?" (Luke 18:8b). Could He appear before us, at anytime during our day, and find us faithfully fulfilling the role to which He has called us? If He came while we were at work, would He find us working hard (Colossians 3:23) and showing integrity in all we do? If He came while we were with our children, would He find us teaching and modeling the Word of God (Deuteronomy 11:19)? If He came during the evening, would He find us exhibiting self-control in our choices of entertainment (Philippians 4:8)? Could He find us sharing the gospel (Matthew 28:19), feeding the poor (Proverbs 22:9), or taking care of widows and orphans (James 1:27)?

We do not need to perform dramatic feats or make ostentatious sacrifices to be ready for the Lord. We simply need to be at our post, doing the work He has called us to do.

–MLG

Prayer

Lord, I thank You that as a Christian, I do not need to fear Your return. I do not want to be ashamed, though, when You come. I want to be found at my post, doing the things that You have set before me. Amen.

For further study ~ Matthew 24:36-51

Am I Ready?

Am I ready for the return of Christ? Am I making wise decisions with my time? What changes might I need to make?

_____

_____

_____

_____

If Christ came back today, what would I like for Him to find me doing?

_____

_____

_____

Soon, one of my God-given tasks will be raising this child. What kind of mother do I want to be?

_____

_____

_____

_____

_Be very careful, then, how you live — not as
unwise but as wise, making the most of every
opportunity, because the days are evil.
Therefore do not be foolish, but understand
what the Lord's will is._
~ Ephesians 5:15-17

Worthy of the Gospel

Whatever happens, conduct yourselves in a manner worthy of the gospel of Christ.
Philippians 1:27

"Okay, I have a couple of questions to ask you," my labor nurse said as she walked in carrying a clipboard. "I know it's hard to talk while you're in labor. You probably don't even like to have to listen to others talking. You'd probably just prefer silence because I know some of those contractions are intense, especially since you haven't taken any drugs. Some women don't mind talking, but some don't like to talk while they're in labor…"

She rambled on as I boiled inside.

"…So what I'm going to do is ask you these questions as quick as possible so you won't have to listen to me for very long…"

Hey, here's an idea. If you stop talking, I won't have to listen to you at all. Then I can concentrate on handling this intense pain that's raging through my body!

That's what I wanted to scream, but I didn't. I managed a few nods to her questions and once in a while asked her to wait until a contraction had passed. Did I exhibit the fruit of kindness? Probably not. Did I show the fruit of gentleness? I don't think so. But, yes, I did demonstrate the fruit of self-control.

I wish I was mature enough that those thoughts would not even enter my mind. I wish I had been an example of kindness, patience, gentleness, and peace. But in the midst of labor, I'm happy for self-control.

James 3:6 says, "The tongue also is a fire, a world of evil among the parts of the body. It corrupts the whole person, sets the whole course of his life on fire, and is itself set on fire by hell." No wonder the tongue is so hard to tame.

Our tongues can be especially wild during pregnancy. Increasing hormones and fatigue are a dangerous combination. We are more tempted to yell at the guy that cut us off on the freeway, humiliate the young clerk that doesn't know how to handle merchandise returns, and tell off the lady in front of us with fifteen items in the express lane.

How can we control our tongue? By recognizing this weakness and daily praying for self-control. By seeing ourselves as representatives of the gospel, no matter what happens. And by changing our outlook on the people around us. "With the tongue we praise our Lord and Father, and with it we curse men, who have been made in God's likeness. Out of the same mouth come praise and cursing. My brothers, this should not be" (James 3:9-10).

The person at whom we are yelling or ridiculing was made in the image of God. She may be a sister in Christ. She may be a lost soul looking for meaning in her life. She may be a desperate woman, crying out inside for the Lord to show her if He is real.

Let's not be a bad testimony to others. Instead, let's show a dying and hopeless world that Christians are different. There is power in the Spirit and we can have the fruit to prove it.

–*MLG*

Prayer

Lord, I carry the gospel with me wherever I go. I want to remember this when I am about to lash out at someone. Please bless my efforts as I begin to show self-control. Amen.

For further study ~ Titus 2:11-14

Do I Live in a Manner Worthy of the Gospel?

In the past week, have I spoken in a way that is a bad testimony to Christ? Is it possible to go back to that person and ask for forgiveness?

_____

_____

_____

_____

To whom do I usually say the things that I regret later? Family members, co-workers, strangers, everyone? Why do I do this? _____

_____

_____

_____

_____

Do I think it is appropriate to verbally assault someone? Who wins when I do that? Who loses? _____

_____

_____

_____

When words are many, sin is not absent,
but he who holds his tongue is wise.
~ Proverbs 10:19

Unwanted Advice

*Let no one deceive you with empty words, for because
of such things God's wrath comes on those who are disobedient.
Therefore, do not be partners with them.*
Ephesians 5:6

There I was riding my bike, enjoying the fresh air, excited to be exercising, when I saw a friend. After our initial greeting, the first words out of his mouth were, "You shouldn't be riding your bike while you're pregnant." I was devastated. I thought about what he had said all the way home. I loved to ride my bike. It was a way I could easily exercise. But I want to do what is best for my baby.

Another day, I was sweeping spider webs from the ceiling of the front porch. Suddenly, my concerned, elderly neighbor came running across the road yelling out to me, "Don't put your hands over your head! You'll wrap the cord around the baby's neck and strangle it!" Her concern calmed a bit when I immediately dropped the broom, but she continued, "Have you had any heartburn? Because if you do it means the baby will have lots of hair."

There is something about pregnancy that solicits advice from those who normally don't care what you do. What are we supposed to do when we get unwanted advice?

God has provided for us a Book of truth. We should compare any advice we receive to the Bible and take it to God in prayer. If we are in the Word regularly it will be easier to recognize what is not true: "See to it that no one takes you captive through hollow and deceptive philosophy, which depends on human tradition and the basic principles of this world rather than on Christ" (Colossians 2:8). This Scripture exhorts *us* to see to it. We are responsible to study His Word so that we'll know the truth.

How are we to respond when others make our business their business? Jesus was a man of compassion yet He never compromised what His Father told Him to do. If we know that riding a bike while pregnant is safe for us, then we can be thankful for the advice but follow the counsel of Scripture, and our doctor or midwife.

There will be times when others question our Christianity or theology. Once again we can turn to God and His Word for the truth. We can also go to our husband, pastors and mature Christians for godly counsel.

Deception is a baited trap. That is why Paul says in Ephesians to not be partners with those who deceive and are disobedient. God has given us what we need to lay a foundation to protect us against deception. When we fill our hearts and minds with God and His Word we will be equipped, ready to discern and not be led astray.

–MK

Prayer

Lord, the world is full of deception and empty lies. Protect me from them as I seek You and study Your Word. Help me discern Your truth as I spend time with You. Equip me to stand up for what is true. Amen.

For further study ~ 2 Timothy 3

Godly Advice

What "old wives' tales" have been told to me?

_____

_____

_____

_____

This is a statement that has been posed to me that I am unsure of:

_____

_____

_____

_____

This is the research I have done to seek God's truth on the subject:

_____

_____

_____

_____

_Rather, we have renounced secret
and shameful ways; we do not use deception,
nor do we distort the word of God.
On the contrary, by setting forth the truth
plainly we commend ourselves to every man's
conscience in the sight of God.
~2 Corinthians 4:2_

Gratefully Nauseated

Do everything without complaining or arguing.
Philippians 2:14

A wave of nausea swept over me. It was followed by another wave, this one a wave of gratefulness. I had begun to spot two days before. Since then I hadn't felt nauseated and my breasts weren't as tender. I began to worry that my pregnancy was going to end in miscarriage. The midwife calmed my fears by assuring me that minimal spotting was quite normal, and all I needed was a little rest.

It's amazing how this spotting changed my perspective on nausea. What was once an ailment to be avoided at all costs now became a comfort as I knew the nausea was a result of hormones — hormones that were helping to support a live and active baby. My circumstances didn't change. It was my perspective and, therefore, my heart that changed.

Under Moses' leadership, God miraculously delivered the Israelites from the slavery of Pharaoh. On the way to the Promised Land, though, they lost sight of God's blessings in the midst of the trials they experienced. Wandering in the desert they were blinded by what they didn't have and what they had left behind. They no longer saw the graciousness that God was extending to them. Most of them never accepted the grace and mercy that God offered. They got caught up in a vicious cycle of grumbling and complaining (the book of Exodus).

There are many unpleasant side effects of pregnancy that we could easily complain about, but Philippians 2:14 encourages us to "Do everything without complaining." This is God's best for us. Does that mean we should try to enjoy the nausea? Of course not. But it does mean we can see it as a continual reminder that God is working to make our babies healthy and strong.

In the midst of sickness we can approach God for mercy and grace to help us in our time of need. We can resist complaining and rejoice in all aspects of our pregnancies. Our amazing God created our bodies to do a miraculous job and we can rejoice that we've been chosen to receive His "little blessings."

–MK

Prayer

Oh, Lord, please change my perspective on the way my body reacts to pregnancy. Help me not to wander in complaints like the Israelites. By their example we learn that this does not please You. My heart wants to please You, Lord. Help me to walk in Your grace and mercy. Amen.

For further study ~ 1 Corinthians 10:1-13

I Am Grateful

What have I complained about during this pregnancy?

_____

_____

_____

_____

_____

This is what I need to do to change my perspective about the side effects of my pregnancy: _____

_____

_____

What can I learn from the Israelites' mistakes? _____

_____

_____

_____

_____

*Let us then approach the throne of grace
with confidence, so that we may receive mercy
and find grace to help us in our time of need.
~ Hebrews 4:16*

The Key to Treasure in Heaven

He will be the sure foundation for your times,
a rich store of salvation and wisdom and knowledge;
the fear of the Lord is the key to this treasure.
Isaiah 33:6

Fear of miscarriage. Fear of birth defects. Fear that we won't live through labor. Fear that we can't afford this child. Pregnancy can be riddled with fear. According to the Bible we are to nurture only a fear of the Lord. It is the beginning of wisdom (Proverbs 9:10) — the key to our treasure.

We treasure many things in this life and we fear what life would be like without these treasures. This reflects a lack of trust in our God, who loves us and works all things for our greatest good (Romans 8:28). "Do not be afraid, little flock, for your Father has been pleased to give you the kingdom. Sell your possessions and give to the poor. Provide purses for yourselves that will not wear out, a treasure in heaven that will not be exhausted, where no thief comes near and no moth destroys. For where your treasure is, there your heart will be also" (Luke 12:32-34).

We are responsible not only for our own treasures, but also for teaching our children to have eternal treasures. Will their lives bring glory to God? Will we share the treasures of heaven with them? These questions can only be answered by God. If we ask them now, though, we can gain direction for aiming our children toward a godly lifestyle.

If we are to give true treasures to our children, we must first have something to give. Are we prepared to point our children to God? Luke 12 encourages us to provide purses that will not wear out, a treasure that will not be exhausted. The only treasure fitting that description is the Creator of all treasures, who is full of wisdom. So when we fear, we are not filling our purses with eternal treasures. Fear wears us out. "Perfect love drives out fear" (1 John 4:18). Therefore the only fear we should cultivate is fear of the Lord. This fear promises wisdom and will never wear out. Can we say the Lord's wisdom is our greatest treasure? If it is, then we can help to make it our child's greatest treasure.

–MK

Prayer

Father, You have given me a precious gift to raise for You. Help me to search for Your treasures so I may share them with my child. Let me present to You a child who loves and serves You with all his heart. Amen.

For Further Study ~ Proverbs 2-3
(The entire book of Proverbs provides an extensive study of wisdom.)

My Key to Treasure in Heaven

What are my greatest fears during this pregnancy?

_____

_____

_____

_____

_____

What insight has God given me to help overcome my fears and develop a godly fear of the Lord?

_____

_____

_____

With what treasures am I filling my purse? Are these treasures I want to share with my child?

_____

_____

_____

_____

_____

By wisdom a house is built,
and through understanding it is established;
through knowledge its rooms are filled with
rare and beautiful treasures.
~ Proverbs 24:3-4

Unbelief and Worry

*"But if you can do anything, take pity on us and help us."
"'If you can'?" said Jesus. "Everything is possible for him
who believes." Immediately the boy's father exclaimed,
"I do believe; help me overcome my unbelief!"*
Mark 9:22-24

No spotting this time. Good. Every time I went to the bathroom I checked for blood. The last thing I wanted was a miscarriage, but it seemed almost like I was expecting it any day.

Why was I worrying so much? If I was going to have a miscarriage I could do nothing to stop it. I could not make this baby stay alive if it was not God's will. If I carry this baby to term, I don't want to look back and see that worrying kept me from experiencing the joy of pregnancy. Nothing good ever comes from worrying.

There are many things that can go wrong in a pregnancy, but there are also many things that can go right. The question is, where will we focus our hearts and minds? We have a choice. We can have peace and joy if we trust that God knows best no matter what happens.

When faced with concerns about a possible miscarriage we want to be like the father in Mark 9:24 who exclaimed, "I do believe; help me overcome my unbelief!" On the other hand, we need to remember that God is sovereign and no matter what happens He makes no mistakes. Theologians have wrestled with these issues, but one thing we can hold onto: though we may not understand God's decisions, we can trust them.

–MK

Prayer

Lord, "I do believe; help me overcome my unbelief!" I want to focus on what is good and right. If my worst fears should be realized, help me to continue to trust in You and stand firm in my faith that You are God and You know what is best for me. Amen.

For further study ~ Romans 4:13-25

Help Me Overcome My Unbelief and Worry

This is what I find difficult to believe God for: _____

_____

_____

_____

_____

Am I exalting a perfect pregnancy above God's will for my life? How have I responded when things haven't gone as I expected?

_____

_____

_____

_____

_____

These are some of the times when I have walked in faith in unbelievable circumstances (use these, Lord, to build my faith): _____

_____

_____

_____

_____

Have faith in the Lord your God and you will be upheld.
~2 Chronicles 20:20

Peace

*He will be like a tree planted by the water
that sends out its roots by the stream. It does not fear when
heat comes; its leaves are always green. It has no worries in a
year of drought and never fails to bear fruit.*
Jeremiah 17:8

Help!

*I rise before dawn and cry for help; I have put
my hope in your word. My eyes stay open through the watches
of the night, that I may meditate on your promises.*
Psalm 119:147 -148

I am so tired. And I am so sick. If I had written the above verses, they would read: "I rise before dawn to throw up and go back to bed. I have put my hope in my pillow. My eyes stay open and I watch television through the night, as I grumble about my lack of sleep."

I am miserable! The last thing I want to do is open up the Bible and read. What I need is sleep and energy. No, what I need is help. "I lift up my eyes to the hills — where does my help come from? My help comes from the Lord, the Maker of heaven and earth" (Psalm 121:1-2).

One of the ways we can receive the Lord's help is through His Word. God's Word is "more precious than gold" (Psalm 19:10). God's Word revives our soul. We are to meditate on His words throughout the day.

But you know that. By reading this book, you are showing that you value Scripture, that you desire to meditate on God's Word, and that you want to apply it to your life. Excellent! Keep up the good work. Now is the time to make this a lifetime habit. You need the Lord's strength now, and you will need it after your baby is born. Learning how to make time for God's Word will greatly benefit you and prepare you for that wonderful day when you finally have that sweet baby in your arms.

When we meditate on God's law, we will be like "a tree planted by streams of water, which yields its fruit in season and whose leaf does not wither" (Psalm 1:3). That's what we want. We want to be a strong tree, withstanding the winds and the rains as we draw our nourishment from the streams of life found in God's Word.

–MLG

Prayer

Lord, I need Your help and I know I can find it in Your Word. May I delight in Your Scriptures and draw nourishment from them. Help me to keep them a priority in my life and not be distracted by other less important things. Amen.

For further study ~ Psalm 19:7-11

Help Me, Lord

Do I delight in the Word of the Lord? What does my daily life show that I delight in?

_____

_____

_____

_____

What, or whom, do I turn to when I am weary?

_____

_____

When is the best time for me to meditate on God's Word? In the morning while I am eating crackers before I get out of bed? In the afternoon while I sip peppermint tea? At night when I am elevating my feet? Am I being consistent in these times? Do I need to change?

_____

_____

_____

_____

Great peace have they who love your law,
and nothing can make them stumble.
~ Psalm 119:165

Waisting Away

Therefore we do not lose heart. Though outwardly we are wasting away, yet inwardly we are being renewed day by day. For our light and momentary troubles are achieving for us an eternal glory that far outweighs them all.
2 Corinthians 4:16-17

My husband smiled at me across the table, waiting patiently for me to begin eating. I ate two bites, then immediately rushed to the sink to lose the two bites. I returned to the table and was greeted by an understanding smile. This was what we expected at dinner. I was losing my waistline, while at the same time wasting half of what I ate, often wishing I could lose more to rid myself of the nausea that followed me wherever I went.

Somehow we all make it through those first months. We are given an assignment: to carry a baby for nine months. Then we are given an obstacle: nausea. Do we resent the challenge?

Some things can't be changed, but we can change our perspective. Nausea is a "light and momentary" trouble that will quickly fade the minute we hold our newborns in our arms.

Our walk with God is like that. We know the kingdom of heaven awaits us but we must go through life facing many obstacles. Some we can avoid, some are unavoidable. This is where character is formed: learning to walk in peace when our circumstances are chaotic.

We may find some comfort in knowing that although hormones cause morning sickness, they also help our bodies to nurture our growing babies. For this we can be thankful. So we endure the miserable side effects, looking ahead to the reward that awaits us: a newborn baby.

It is the same in the circumstances we face throughout life. Ultimately, we know God is doing a mighty work for our greatest good. There may be unpleasant side effects at this time, but we have peace in God that He is building our character for eternity.

–MK

Prayer

Thank You, Lord, for the unpleasant circumstances in life that draw me closer to You. Thank You for Your peace to face whatever is set before me. Amen.

For further study ~ Isaiah 26:1-13

Waisting Away/Awaiting Reward

What side effects from this pregnancy have been most difficult to endure so far? _____

_____

_____

_____

_____

How have I responded to the difficulties of pregnancy? Is this also how I respond to the difficulties of my life? _____

_____

_____

_____

_____

Knowing that there is an eternal reward waiting for me, how can I respond to the challenges in my life?

_____

_____

_____

_____

Let the peace of Christ rule in your hearts, since as members of one body you were called to peace. And be thankful.
~ Colossians 3:15

Fear of the Lord

*Charm is deceptive, and beauty is fleeting;
but a woman who fears the Lord is to be praised.*
Proverbs 31:30

I looked at the pregnancy test laying on my bathroom counter. Yes, it was definitely positive. I turned and walked out of the bathroom to tell my family the good news, when…pow! One million fat cells burst forth and clung to my body in a solid five-pound mass.

At least I feel like that is what happens. My body stores up enough fat to support three babies with each pregnancy. Just a glance through my photo album and you can instantly see when I was pregnant: I'm carrying at least an extra ten pounds, and that's just in my face! Proverbs 31:30 says beauty is fleeting; I say mine is fleeing!

Let's look again at the Scripture above. It shows that we are not to be seeking praise for our charm and our beauty. Instead, it is our fear of the Lord that will bring us true praise. The fear of the Lord seems an odd contrast to charm and beauty, but further study reveals the connection. An emphasis on charm and beauty is based on what? It is based on wanting to look good to others, worrying about what others think, using some man-made definition of beauty to establish our personal goals. In other words, it is based on the fear of man. Our goal should be the complete opposite: the fear of the Lord.

What is the fear of the Lord? Proverbs 8:13 defines it as hating evil, hating pride, hating arrogance, hating evil behavior, and hating perverse speech. These are the qualities in a woman that will be praised, not all of our work on external beauty and charm.

Scripture not only says we will be praised for developing a fear of the Lord, it also lists several other benefits. The fear of the Lord is the beginning of wisdom (Proverbs 9:10) and the beginning of knowledge (Proverbs 1:7). The fear of the Lord leads to life (Proverbs 19:23) and it is a fountain of life (Proverbs 14:27). These are eternal attributes. These are what we need as mothers. "He who fears the Lord has a secure fortress, and for his children it will be a refuge" (Proverbs 14:26).

–MLG

Prayer

Lord, please help me to establish godly goals for my life. May I not be distracted by the external and the temporal. As I watch my body change during this pregnancy, help me to not be discouraged, but to instead focus on the fruit You are developing in my heart. Amen.

For further study ~ 2 Corinthians 5

Whom Do I Fear?

When I worry about how I look, who comes to mind? Is there someone else's opinion that I am elevating above God's?

_____

_____

_____

_____

_____

I want to be faithful to take care of my body. Are there any ways in my life that I have allowed this responsibility to supersede more important ones?

_____

_____

_____

Here are some ways that I see the fear of others has affected my thinking during this pregnancy: _____

_____

_____

_____

_____

_____

Fear of man will prove to be a snare,
but whoever trusts in the Lord is kept safe.
~ Proverbs 29:25

How Can I Be a Mommy?

Forgetting what is behind and straining toward what is ahead, I press on toward the goal to win the prize for which God has called me heavenward in Christ Jesus.
Philippians 3:13-14

Lord, how am I going to be a mommy? Don't You remember all those things I've done? Don't you see me now? I can be impatient and selfish, and sometimes I just choose to do what I know is wrong. I can't even get my own life together, so how can I raise this child?

Do you think this is the attitude God wants us to have? Does He want us to hold on to the sins that He has forgiven? "As far as the east is from the west, so far has he removed our transgressions from us" (Psalm 103:12). God sent His one and only Son to die for our sins so that we could receive forgiveness. He made this sacrifice so that we could be free from our sins, not paralyzed by them.

It is the enemy who wants us to carry around our sins. It is the enemy who tries to convince us that we need to pay for our own sins with a lifetime of regret. "Godly sorrow brings repentance that leads to salvation and leaves no regret, but worldly sorrow brings death" (2 Corinthians 7:10). When we confess our sins to the Lord, we are forgiven, and we need to walk in that freedom so that we can fully devote ourselves to what God has called us to do today.

The seventh chapter of Luke records a beautiful story of the Lord's heart toward those who come to Him in repentance. Jesus was dining at a Pharisee's house when a "sinful woman" came in. She sat at Jesus' feet, anointed His feet with her tears and perfume, and then wiped His feet with her hair. The guests at the dinner were appalled, but Jesus said to her, "Your sins are forgiven. Your faith has saved you; go in peace" (Luke 7:48 and 50).

Jesus told her to go in peace, not to carry the burden of her sins with her. Not to earn His forgiveness by being mournful enough. Not to make up for her sins with good works. No, His forgiveness was instant and complete, giving her the peace to go on.

This is what our Father offers us. Many of us have difficulty understanding this kind of forgiveness because we grew up in homes where it was not modeled. We were forgiven only when we finally seemed sorry enough, and even then, forgiveness was often never complete because love and favor were withheld from us as a form of punishment.

Our heavenly Father offers us complete forgiveness and unconditional love when we come to Him in repentance. Let's not allow anything to stop us from receiving this — not our experiences from the past or our sins. Let's look forward to the opportunity of raising a child, knowing that the Lord has given us a clean slate, and He will be with us every step of the way.

–MLG

Prayer

Lord, I do not want to be trapped in my past, or trapped in my sins. Please set me free. I want to raise this child with the hope and confidence that comes from You. Amen.

For further study ~ Psalm 103

I Can Be a Mommy

When I am reminded of my past failures, how can I respond? Thank the Lord that I am no longer trapped in those sins? Quote scriptures on forgiveness? How can I use my memories of sin as triggers for good?

_____

_____

_____

Who has modeled true forgiveness to me?

_____

_____

_____

_____

Have I been modeling true forgiveness to those around me? Or am I in any way still trying to make others pay for the things they've done?

_____

_____

_____

_____

But if you do not forgive men their sins,
your Father will not forgive your sins.
~ Matthew 6:15

Even If He Does Not

But even if he does not, we want you to know,
O king, that we will not serve your gods or worship
the image of gold you have set up.
Daniel 3:18

The contractions were coming four minutes apart as I paced in the hospital lobby, trying to wait as long as I could before officially checking in. The pain was intense. It's worth it, I kept telling myself, because today I get to hold my baby.

Suddenly, my knees went weak as a pain gripped me — this time in my heart. Passing right in front of me were several hospital aides pulling wagons. And in each wagon sat a pale little child. Each of the them was bald, with tubes in his or her head and throughout their tiny bodies. Some of the little ones looked up at me as I stared with tears pouring down my face.

Oh, Lord, I cried inside. Please give me a healthy baby. Their mothers were once standing outside the delivery room, too, full of hopes and dreams for their children and their lives together. Dreams of running and playing, beaches and roller coasters, parties and weddings. Lord, these children are so sick. Many are dying. I know they are a blessing to their mothers. I know their mothers love them. But Lord, the heartbreak must be overwhelming.

And then I realized. Each of those mothers must have been like me, crying out for a healthy baby. Yet, that is not what they got.

There I stood. I did not know what was waiting for me as I stepped through those doors to deliver my baby. But what I did know was a powerful passage from the third chapter of Daniel. Shadrach, Meshach and Abednego were about to be thrown into a blazing furnace because they were worshipping the Lord. They had no idea what would happen in those flames. But these three men boldly declared that the Lord was able to save them. And even if He did not, they would still worship only the Lord.

I knew that I, too, must make that decision as I stood outside the delivery room. God was able to give me a perfectly formed and healthy baby, but even if He did not, I would still worship only Him.

Our praise is not based on circumstances. Each baby is born with a purpose, and we cannot use our own limited understanding to evaluate a life. Consider Job. He lost all his possessions, all his children, and he was covered in painful sores. Yet he responded, "Shall we accept good from God, and not trouble?" (Job 2:10).

He is not Lord because we acknowledge Him during the good times. He is Lord of the universe whether we choose to praise Him or not. Isaiah 64:8 says, "Yet, O Lord, you are our Father. We are the clay, you are the potter; we are all the work of your hand." We may not understand why He allows handicaps in some children. We may not understand how He forms us, or even why our lives take a certain shape. But either way, He is still the potter. He is still the Lord. He is still worthy of our praise (1 Chronicles 16:25).

Some days are going to be harder than others to praise the Lord. But we have this comfort: He is not only an omnipotent God, He is a good God. Even when our lives are not what we expected or hoped for, we can know for sure that "in all things God works for the good of those who love him, who have been called according to his purpose" (Romans 8:28).

–MLG

Prayer

Lord, I want to praise You in all things, no matter what my circumstances. You are the Lord, yesterday, today and tomorrow. My baby is in Your hands, and I ask for a healthy child. Please prepare me for whatever this child will bring into my life, and help me to worship You through it all. Amen.

For further study ~ Psalm 23

Even When He Does Not

When was a time in my life when I didn't understand why something happened, but I can now see how God worked it out for my good?

_____

_____

_____

I've read Psalm 16:8, Psalm 45:6 and Revelation 1:8. These verses show me that:

_____

_____

_____

If I did not worship and serve the Lord, what would be my hope in life?

_____

_____

_____

But if serving the Lord seems undesirable to you, then choose for yourselves this day whom you will serve... But as for me and my household, we will serve the Lord.
~ Joshua 24:15

Choices

Submit to God and be at peace with him;
in this way prosperity will come to you.
Job 22:21

Doctors, midwives, hospitals, birthing centers, home birth. The options for delivery seemed endless. I was in a new town, with a new insurance company. I talked on the phone with one office and thought, I could use these people to deliver my baby. Then my family and I visited a birthing center and we were convinced we could do that as well. Two days later I visited another place that I also liked. How would I ever decide?

Because I was new to the area I had to trust total strangers to help me bring my baby into the world. What a step of faith it is to trust God to lead me where I need to go! By the time my baby comes, my prayer is that a good relationship will be established with my doctor or midwife.

Proverbs 4:11-12 says, "I guide you in the way of wisdom and lead you along straight paths. When you walk, your steps will not be hampered; when you run, you will not stumble." As we walk into each office or hospital, we can ask God, "Is this the place where You want my baby delivered and are these the people You want to assist me?" God is faithful to let us know the path we should take. With all of the malpractice and scary stories you hear it is only in God that we find peace in our decisions.

One thing we can count on: wherever we decide to deliver our baby, God will be with us. He was there at conception; He will be there at birth. He will be full of compassion if there are any complications, and He will be rejoicing with us if everything goes well. When we are submitted to God, we will prosper, not always in the world's way, but always in God's way.

–MK

Prayer

Lord Jesus, show me the path I am to take in choosing the place to deliver my baby and the people to assist me. Show me through circumstances and counsel, but more importantly, show me through Your peace. I trust You with my baby, the birth process and the people and place You lead me to. Amen.

For further study ~ Psalm 143:5-10

My Choices

This is the place that I felt God's peace to deliver my baby and the name of my doctor or midwife:

_____

_____

This is how I knew that this was the place and these were the people that God was leading me to:

_____

_____

_____

_____

This is an area where I lack peace and my prayer to God as I seek His peace:

_____

_____

_____

_____

_____

A heart at peace gives life to the body.
~ Proverbs 14:30

Shadow of Death

Even though I walk through the valley of the shadow of death, I will fear no evil, for you are with me; your rod and your staff, they comfort me.
Psalm 23:4

I stood in the emergency room with my husband and my pastor. We were praying for my eleven-year-old. She had arrived by ambulance after my husband and I found her in bed unconscious and not breathing.

As I stood there praying, I was convicted of my recent thoughts concerning the baby in my womb: If I can just get through the first trimester, then my baby will be okay. I was so worried about keeping my unborn baby safe, I forgot that at any moment God could call a child home, no matter what her age.

Many families have walked through the deep sorrow of losing a child. God's grace is always present and carries them through their darkest hour. I have some friends who lost their eight-month-old son in a drowning accident. I was deeply moved when I saw them at their son's funeral praising God. Their ability to give Him glory in such tragic circumstances can be attributed only to the grace of God in their lives. They communicated God's grace and faithfulness to others, and shared how the prayers and support of the body of Christ carried them through their darkest hour.

Just before their son died, my friends had a ceremony in the hospital room dedicating him to God. As short as his life was, it was priceless. His life made a tremendous impact on our entire church and people throughout our city.

My eleven-year-old had experienced a seizure, which is usually not fatal. But in that instant when I found her not responding to me, I thought she was dying. Even amidst the panic, God's hand was in every circumstance throughout that trial. I prayed continuously and His peace enveloped me as I walked through the valley of the shadow of death.

We still have our daughter with us. Our friends have only memories of their son. Both children were, and still are, in God's hands, each of their days numbered. Both of our families found peace and comfort as God carried us through fearful and unknown circumstances. We continue with life, different than we were before, yet knowing that every day is a gift from God.

–MK

Prayer

Sovereign God, I give my child to You. You have given me this blessing and I am grateful for every day You allow me to raise her. I pray for a long life, yet at the same time I hold this life loosely knowing You have loaned this baby to me to raise for Your glory. Amen.

For further study ~ Psalm 28:6-9

God's Shadow of Peace

Here is my prayer dedicating this child to God:

_____

_____

_____

_____

Here is a difficult circumstance that the peace of God carried me through:

_____

_____

Here is my prayer for a family member or a friend who has lost a child. Or, here is my prayer to God as I recall the circumstances surrounding the death of my child:

_____

_____

_____

_____

_____

I will praise you, O Lord my God, with all my heart; I will glorify your name forever. For great is your love toward me; you have delivered me from the depths of the grave.
~ Psalm 86:12-13

Peaceful Pregnancy

*You will keep in perfect peace him whose mind is
steadfast, because he trusts in you. Trust in the Lord forever,
for the Lord, the Lord, is the Rock eternal.*
Isaiah 26:3-4

I called to wish my mother a happy birthday and update my parents on my pregnancy. My dad answered the phone and informed me that my brother had died of a sudden heart attack. I was shocked as I tried to accept this devastating news.

Full of sorrow, I began to prepare for the trip to my hometown for the funeral. I went to my previously scheduled obstetrician's appointment to make sure it was safe to travel. So many questions and worries filled my mind: Not only did I have to face the sorrow that gripped my heart, but I was concerned how this stress would affect my baby. My doctor reassured me that grieving would not harm my baby or make her a sorrowful child. I was then able to set aside worry and face the situation.

Pregnancy is normally a joyous experience. There are times, though, when life throws us an unexpected turn. Our joy can be overshadowed by grief, anxieties, or tragic circumstances. God's peace is there for us, especially in the darkest hour. It is at times like these that we need to run to Him. He is the only strength that will carry us through — our Rock eternal. Because of Him, we can have a mind that is steadfast and peaceful, even when life is difficult.

Again, we draw comfort from Isaiah: "'Though the mountains be shaken and the hills be removed, yet my unfailing love for you will not be shaken nor my covenant of peace be removed,' says the Lord, who has compassion on you. All your sons will be taught by the Lord, and great will be your children's peace" (Isaiah 54:10 and 13).

God promises His peace and compassionate love for us even in the most challenging circumstances. When our world is shaken, we find our comfort only in God, who will not be shaken.

–MK

Prayer

Father God, You promise to be there to help me to walk in Your perfect peace when my world is shaken. Help me to keep my mind steadfast as I trust in You and stand firm on Your rock. I want to lead my children by example and bring them Your comfort. Amen.

For further study: Isaiah 61

(This is the encouragement God gave my brother's widow as she sought Him for peace.)

Peace in My Pregnancy

What circumstance or anxiety has shaken me during this pregnancy?

_____

_____

_____

_____

This is how God showed me His peace and unfailing love:

_____

_____

_____

_____

_____

Here is my prayer to God to help me through any "mountains" that have shaken this pregnancy:

_____

_____

_____

_____

The Lord gives strength to his people;
the Lord blesses his people with peace.
~ Psalm 29:11

Goodness

And we pray this in order that you may live a life worthy of the Lord and may please him in every way: bearing fruit in every good work, growing in the knowledge of God.

Colossians 1:10

Doing Good

*Therefore, as we have opportunity, let us do good to
all people, especially to those who belong to the family of believers.*
Galatians 6:10

"Kim called and offered to bring us dinner on Sunday," my husband whispered after he opened the door to our bedroom and saw that I was awake. I had been in bed the past two hours, trying to get rid of a migraine headache. This additional pain only increased the nausea and vomiting I had from pregnancy. I felt almost delirious from discomfort.

"I hope you said no," I managed to respond.

"Not at all," my husband said cheerfully. "I said we would appreciate the help."

I could not believe Kim was going to bring us a meal. Kim, who was pregnant herself. Kim, whose nausea and vomiting was so bad that in the early stage of her pregnancy she was forced to get shots a couple of times each week. This woman was going to make a meal for me?

I could not think of one thing I'd done for someone else since I'd gotten pregnant. This conclusion reveals my biggest struggle when I'm pregnant— apathy and self-absorption. I just want to lie around and do nothing. I realize that God's grace and mercy are strong upon us during pregnancy, and it is vital that we take care of ourselves and the baby in our womb. But Galatians 6:10 says we are to do good "as we have opportunity." Certainly there are some opportunities for us to do good while we are pregnant.

Maybe taking a meal to someone is just too much right now. Perhaps we could bring a plate of cookies to a neighbor, even if it is just the slice-and-bake kind. Hosting a six-couple dinner party may not be best during this season, but maybe we could invite a friend over to watch a movie with us. Or now might be the time to invite a lonely co-worker out for lunch—just choose a restaurant that's easy on your fickle stomach!

Galatians 6:2 says, "Carry each other's burdens, and in this way you will fulfill the law of Christ." This is an excellent season to be praying for others. We need to be resting anyway, so prayer is a perfect activity. Plus, it will help keep our minds off ourselves. We could even keep a stack of notecards handy and jot a line or two to a friend to let her know we've been praying for her.

We could also take advantage of our expanding waistline. As we are putting maternity clothes in our closet, it is a great time to take out any clothes that we don't think we'll wear again. If you don't know someone to give these clothes to, call a charitable organization to come and pick them up.

Some of these ideas may sound great to you. Some may sound unrealistic. That's fine, but we need to be open to whatever opportunities the Lord is placing before us to do good to others. God can still use us, even now.

–MLG

Prayer

Father, I don't want to spend these nine months focusing only on myself. Open my eyes to the needs around me, and help me to see which ones I can meet. Protect me, though, from taking on more than I should. Help me to make wise choices with my time, keeping in mind my responsibility to this baby. Amen.

For further study ~ 2 Corinthians 9:6-15

What Good Can I Do?

Here are some ways that I have been blessed by others:

_____

_____

_____

_____

What ways could I serve others during this pregnancy?

_____

_____

_____

_____

Is there anything I'm doing now, or involved in, that I believe God wants me to stop doing, and focus on something better for this season of life?

_____

_____

_____

_____

For we are God's workmanship,
created in Christ Jesus to do good works,
which God prepared in advance for us to do.
~ Ephesians 2:10

Buried Treasure

For you are a people holy to the Lord your God.
The Lord your God has chosen you out of all the peoples on
the face of the earth to be his people, his treasured possession.
Deuteronomy 7:6

Prophecies concerning her child were given centuries before the conception, during pregnancy, upon birth and throughout her child's life. "But Mary treasured up all these things and pondered them in her heart" (Luke 2:19). Her son was fully God (John 1:1) and fully man (John 1:14), yet Mary and Joseph were given the charge to raise this young man who was about to change the world forever!

Mary encouraged her son to step out in His first miracle (John 2), and followed Him throughout his ministry (Acts 1:14). Mary watched her son suffer for the sake of this sinful world (John 19:25) as she stood at the foot of the cross. Mary witnessed her son fulfill His purpose in this world (John 19:30).

Our children are also created for God's purposes. While no human could ever come close to the accomplishments of Christ, each life is important to God. Throughout the lives of our children, we will be given glimpses into their personalities and talents. Using the wisdom from the Bible, we can gently and firmly guide them to fulfill their callings.

The babies in our wombs are treasures, and God will give us maps. Sometimes the directions are clear, sometimes a little hazy. But through prayer and God's Word, we will have the wisdom we need to raise our children to serve Him. We can even begin seeking God's direction for our babies now.

We will be different because of the birth of our baby. Yet we are not the only ones affected. Every smile they give to others in the grocery store is a precious jewel. Every act of obedience proves God's wisdom is golden to a disobedient world. Every tender gesture shines the light of Christ like diamonds glistening on black velvet. What is buried in our wombs is a treasure waiting to bring forth a bright ray of hope, not only to us, but also to the world.

–MK

Prayer

Thank You, Sovereign God, for this treasure You have given me. What a challenging, yet rewarding job lays ahead of me. Lord, show me how to raise this child and unearth the treasure within him. Show me how to prepare him to fulfill his role in this world. Amen.

For further study ~ Deuteronomy 26:17-18

Digging for My Buried Treasure

How can I prepare myself to unearth the godly treasure buried
in my child?

_____

_____

_____

_____

_____

What can I ponder in my heart about this treasure being formed
in my womb?

_____

_____

Do I see myself as God's treasured possession? What things may have
hindered me from grasping the full extent of God's love?

_____

_____

_____

_____

_____

*And if you look for it as silver
and search for it as for hidden treasure,
then you will understand the fear of the
Lord and find the knowledge of God.
~ Proverbs 2:4-5*

The Goodness Guarantee

For everything God created is good, and nothing
is to be rejected if it is received with thanksgiving, because
it is consecrated by the word of God and prayer.
1 Timothy 4:4-5

Entering into the second trimester, I began to breathe a sigh of relief. It looked as though this pregnancy was free and clear of problems. If I was going to miscarry it probably would have happened by now. What else could go wrong? This was my first child and I felt great!

Lying on the examining table for the first sonogram, I excitedly listened while the doctor mumbled, "There's the heartbeat…baby is progressing in size at the appropriate stage…placenta…well, it looks as though you have placenta previa."

"What's that?" I asked.

The doctor explained that my placenta was partially covering the birth canal. If it didn't move by the time of delivery I would need a Cesarean section. At this point it was not life-threatening, but I was not allowed to lift anything, do any heavy cleaning, vacuum, or have intercourse. Any of these could promote a miscarriage. The doctor reassured me that if I took the necessary precautions, the chances were good that I would have a healthy baby right on schedule.

Just when I thought it was safe to breathe a sigh of relief, I had to face the reality that there are no guarantees in this life. God, I thought, how could You do this to me?

Psalm 119:68 gives us comfort. "You are good, and what you do is good; teach me your decrees." Our God is a good God. The babies He has given us are His blessings. The only guarantee we have in this life is that God is good. Should we worry away our entire pregnancy with the fear that God does not have us and our babies in His hands? Should we not receive all news from God with thanksgiving? If the worst case scenario happens, will God cease being good? "You are forgiving and good, O Lord, abounding in love to all who call to you" (Psalm 86:5). Our only response is to consecrate our babies to God by His word and prayer (1 Timothy 4:5).

In the eighth month of my pregnancy, the baby dropped below the placenta. Three weeks later I delivered a normal, healthy baby. Just to further show God's faithfulness, that placenta was stuck good and tight in my uterus. The doctor had to work to pull it out.

No matter what the outcome, God is still a good God. He is good in that He chooses the circumstances that are best for our lives and our babies'. Not because we get what we think is best, but because God does what is truly best.

–MK

Prayer

Lord, You are good. Your love endures forever; Your faithfulness continues through all generations (Psalm 100:5). Your goodness reaches into my life and my baby's life. Help me to trust You in every circumstance of my pregnancy. Help me to meditate on Your goodness when things seem good and when things do not seem good. You are the only guarantee in this life. Let me hold on to nothing but You. Amen.

For Further Study ~1 Peter 3:13-15

My Claim to the Goodness Guarantee

How has God shown me His goodness in this pregnancy?

_____

_____

_____

_____

_____

_____

How have I responded to an incident when things have not seemed good?

_____

_____

_____

_____

How could I have responded differently?

_____

_____

_____

_____

_The Lord is good to all; he has
compassion on all he has made._
~ Psalm 145:9

Living in the Light

*For you were once darkness, but now you are
light in the Lord. Live as children of light.*
Ephesians 5:8

When you walk into a dark room, you see only a few basic shapes and shadows. No details are evident, and there is a lot in the room that you're not even aware of. Switch on the light, though, and the things in the room instantly become visible.

The Bible calls sin the "deeds of darkness" (Romans 13:12). As Christians, we are to live in the light—no dark corners where we do the things we shouldn't. We are to live in such a way that the light brings us security, not shame.

We know that God sees everything, but we fool ourselves into believing that it doesn't always matter what we do. We can think that as long as we are doing what's right most of the time, we deserve a break once in a while to just "be ourselves and relax." Sometimes that involves plopping down and watching a television show that glamorizes immorality. It may be talking on the phone with a friend and telling her all the juicy gossip from work, or listening to her gossip. It could be snapping at our husbands after a rough day.

Do we lower our moral standards around close friends or family? Do we try to keep certain parts of our life hidden from others? The Bible issues us a strong warning: "Woe to those who go to great depths to hide their plans from the Lord, who do their work in darkness and think, 'Who sees us? Who will know?'" (Isaiah 29:15). Do we need help remembering that God sees everything we do?

Great news! God is sending us help—sending it to us in the form of a little baby. We may not recognize the help right away, but by the time our babies are about nine months old, we'll realize what the Lord has done. He has sent us a mirror. That's right! Our precious little babies will soon start imitating us. It is so cute—at first. Putting on hats, looking at books, wearing our shoes. But then their vocabulary kicks in. We hear words pop out of their mouths that make us cringe. We discover our children playing phone and dramatically repeating the phrase, "Did you know…?" We secretly watch as they play house, and are shocked to see how the "mommy" talks to the "daddy." And this is only in the early years, before our children get old enough to begin questioning our actions with penetrating observations.

Having children will shine a new light on our lives. Sounds a little scary, doesn't it? We don't need to dread this illumination, though. Darkness is a trap and a deception. Nothing is hidden from the Lord, and we will just get further lost in the darkness if we try to hide our sin from others. Our babies are gifts from God that will help us see ourselves better, repent when we need to, and live in the light.

–MLG

Prayer

Lord, I don't want to be striving to keep parts of my life secret. I want to do the good things that please You, whether anyone on earth sees me or not. When I do sin, I want to be quick to confess it, so that I'll have nothing to hide and I won't need to fear the light. Amen.

For further study ~ Ephesians 5:1-21

I Want to Live in the Light

Are there things in my life that I try to hide from others, or from God? If so, what are they?

_____

_____

_____

Why would I try to keep some things in the dark corners of my life? Is it pride? Is it a lack of understanding of God's Word?

_____

_____

_____

_____

If I repent to God for these things, I can have the freedom to walk into the light. Will I do that today? Who else do I need to ask to forgive me?

_____

_____

_____

_____

When Jesus spoke again to the people,
he said, "I am the light of the world.
Whoever follows me will never walk in
darkness, but will have the light of life."
~ John 8:12

Belonging to God

Do you not know that your body is a temple of the Holy Spirit, who is in you, whom you have received from God? You are not your own; you were bought at a price. Therefore honor God with your body.
1 Corinthians 6:19-20

"And right here," said the obstetrician as he pointed to the blurry image on the sonogram screen, "is where we usually see a heartbeat."

"Usually?" I managed to whisper in spite of the pain gripping my heart as I lay motionless on the examining table.

"Yes, usually," the doctor responded. "But as you can see here, there is no heartbeat. I'm sorry."

Tears silently flowed down my cheeks. I looked up at my husband's face, contorted in sorrow and compassion. I looked over at the faces of my young children, staring at me in confusion, anxiously waiting for me to explain what was said about their baby brother or sister.

"The doctor says our baby has no heartbeat," I began, "which means our baby has died."

I continued on, though I was now sobbing as I spoke. "Mommy and Daddy trust God and we know that our baby is in His hands and we'll see our baby in heaven. We are crying, though, because we just wish we could have had our baby with us longer."

My children were comforted by these words, and I was, too. Yes, that is what I believe. I trust God. I trust Him with my life and the life that was growing within me. He paid a high price for me when He sent His Son to die on the cross for my sins. I accepted His offer of forgiveness and now my life is not my own. My heart and soul belong to Him. My body belongs to Him. My womb belongs to Him.

And to what kind of God do we belong? We belong to a faithful God who "watches over all who love him" (Psalm 145:20). We belong to a compassionate God who has "put [our] tears in [His] bottle" (Psalm 56:8). We belong to a loving God who in all things "works for the good of those who love him" (Romans 8:28).

Does that mean we understand everything that happens? Certainly not. "'For my thoughts are not your thoughts, neither are your ways my ways,' declares the Lord" (Isaiah 55:8). May we willingly place our wombs in the hands of God, knowing that His ways are right (Hosea 14:9).

–MLG

Prayer

Please bless my baby and keep him safe. May he be born healthy and strong. But Lord, my womb is Yours, and I am thankful to be a part of Your eternal plan. I know that no matter what tomorrow holds, my baby and I are in Your hands. Amen.

For further study ~ Job 1

I Belong to God

Do I believe my womb belongs to God? What are ways (thoughts, words, or actions) I have been using to wrestle with God for control of my womb?

_____

_____

_____

_____

_____

In what way does knowing I belong to a powerful and loving God affect the way I live?

_____

_____

_____

_____

Do I trust God with my womb and the life inside it?

_____

_____

"For I know the plans I have for you, declares the Lord, plans to prosper you and not to harm you, plans to give you hope and a future."
~ Jeremiah 29:11

What a Gift!

Every good and perfect gift is from above, coming down from the Father of the heavenly lights.
James 1:17

When I was 11 years old, I would rush home from school, toss my books down, and run next door. I would spend the next couple of hours picking weeds, washing windows, cleaning, and vacuuming for my elderly neighbor. Then I would hurry back, minutes before it was time for my mother to arrive home from work.

This went on for a couple of weeks, and at the end of each day, my neighbor would pay me exactly the rate I requested: "a penny a minute." It was December and I was saving for something very special—a clock radio for my mother. I had seen one in a catalog, but my own meager savings fell far short of the price. So I secretly worked until I had enough money.

I eagerly counted down the days until Christmas. I could barely think of anything else except that clock radio. In fact, all I remember about that Christmas season is my own excitement about giving my mother such a wonderful gift.

Do you know that right now someone is lovingly preparing a special gift for you? The almighty, powerful God of the universe, the Ruler of all ages, is delicately creating a baby for you. The Bible says that God is knitting your baby together in your womb (Psalm 139:13). The Father and Creator of all is tenderly forming your baby's eyes, nose, and mouth. He has chosen the color of her eyes, the texture of her hair, the curve in her smile. Even more than that, He is creating your baby in His own image (Genesis 1:27).

We know that ultimately our babies belong to the Lord. But He has chosen to give them to us for a season. He has chosen to form these wonderful gifts in our wombs, to let us feel the movements of our little babies, to one day hold our precious bundles in our arms, and feel their soft skin, their gentle breathing, and their warmth as they snuggle into us. Oh, how the Lord must anxiously await the day we finally give birth and get to see our marvelous gifts.

–MLG

Prayer

Father, thank You so much for blessing me with this baby. I can't wait to see my baby and hold her in my arms. May I always remember that she is a gift from You. Amen.

For further study ~ Psalm 89:1-18

My Gift from God

When I think about the birth of my baby, what comes to mind?

_____

_____

_____

_____

Am I allowing anything to steal the joy of anticipating my baby's birth?
If so, what is it?

_____

_____

_____

_____

Father, here is my prayer of thanks for this precious gift:

_____

_____

_____

_____

_____

_____

_The Lord will indeed give what is good,
and our land will yield its harvest._
~ _Psalm 85:12_

Always Hungry

Let them give thanks to the Lord for his unfailing
love and his wonderful deeds for men, for he satisfies the
thirsty and fills the hungry with good things.
Psalm 107:8-9

I stepped off the scale in shock. If I remembered correctly, I weighed about this much at the *end* of my last pregnancy. I wasn't even half way through this one! My baby only weighed about a pound. The problem must be with my eating habits. My nausea had passed, so I had begun eating enough for two, possibly even three. I was constantly hungry. I couldn't let my baby starve, so I ate, and I ate whenever I was hungry, which seemed to be all the time. It's no wonder I gained so much!

Jesus promised that if we hunger and thirst for righteousness we will be filled (Matthew 5:6). In John 6:35 He declared, "I am the bread of life. He who comes to me will never go hungry, and he who believes in me will never be thirsty." This analogy is used in Scripture to teach us to seek after God. Do we hunger for God as we hunger for food? Do we constantly crave more and more of God? We eat daily—on average, three times a day. Do we seek God that often? How can we seek God that often?

When we desire to eat healthy foods, it takes preparation. So it is with our spiritual diet. We want to make the Word of God as available as possible. We can do this by considering our lifestyle, planning time in the Word, and strategically placing Scripture.

Here are some ideas to get you started:

- Stick a verse on your refrigerator.
- Put one on the dashboard of your car.
- Tape one on your bathroom mirror.
- Place one next to your computer.
- Set a regular time aside each day to study the Word.
- Take advantage of walking time to meditate on what you've studied.

• Listen to praise or teaching tapes during your commutes.

These are just examples. As you pray, God will show you creative ways to spend time with Him. He desires fellowship with us and we can be confident that if we ask, He will provide the nourishment we need.

–MK

Prayer

Jesus, You promise that if I believe in You I will never go hungry because You are the Bread of Life! Thank You for filling me everyday with Your perfect nourishment. Help me to live my life for You, always looking for opportunities to be with You. Amen.

For further study ~ Revelation 7:15-17

Satisfying My Hunger for Jesus

This is how much weight I have gained:_____

Week of pregnancy:_____

In what ways have I been hungering and thirsting for God? Do I hunger for food more than I hunger for God?

_____

_____

_____

_____

_____

_____

How can meditating on God's eternal promises help me to live day to day?

_____

_____

_____

_____

_____

_____

Blessed are you who hunger now, for you will be satisfied.
~ Luke 6:21

Deadline Dead End

But Jesus often withdrew to lonely places and prayed.
Luke 5:16

I was working on a project at home with the deadline approaching too quickly for comfort. My headache was getting worse and I could barely concentrate on the computer screen. I tried to push on, but to no avail. I was up against a wall and could go no further without God's direction. My head was pounding. I had to set this project aside for the baby's sake, if not my own.

Lying in my darkened bedroom I cried out to God: "This is a project You want me to do. It needs to be done by the deadline. I am stuck and can't go any further. Help me, Lord."

I was lying there, capable of doing nothing else so I called on God. He is my refuge when I am distressed. Then God began to formulate the next step in my mind. When I awoke hours later, my headache had almost subsided and I was able to pursue the direction God had given me.

We get caught up in the demands of life. These things should not take away our devotion to God, but sadly enough they often do. The Lord is faithful and allows trials that draw us to Him so we will not forget our total dependence on Him. He is the one who allows us to do projects in the first place. He is the one who gives us our talents and capabilities. He is the reason we take our next breath. Why is it when the going gets tough, often the first thing we forget is our Source?

Jesus' time was continually in demand. He was followed by masses of people wanting to hear Him teach. He was sought after continually. Yet we see throughout Scripture that He withdrew from the multitudes to seek His Father in private (Mark 1:35).

We need to follow Jesus' example and regularly withdraw for direction and renewal from God. He is the strength that keeps us going. When deadlines are looming ahead and the stresses of life are pressing in, we need to take the time to run to God. It will be time well spent. Our projects will turn out better. And our babies will benefit because Mom will be peaceful and we will be satisfied with a job well done.

–MK

Prayer

Lord, forgive me when the distractions of this life draw my focus away from You. Let me never forget that without You, I can accomplish nothing. You are my Strength and my Source. You are my all in all. Amen.

For further study ~ Psalm 20

Deadline Dead End

What has distracted me from spending time with God?

_____

_____

_____

_____

_____

How has this affected me and/or my pregnancy?

_____

_____

_____

_____

After withdrawing to seek God, how has He changed my attitude in regard to the distractions of my life?

_____

_____

_____

_____

_____

Answer me when I call to you, O my righteous God. Give me relief from my distress; be merciful to me and hear my prayer.
~ Psalm 4:1

Kindness

I no longer call you servants, because a servant does not know his master's business. Instead, I have called you friends, for everything that I learned from my Father I have made known to you. You did not choose me, but I chose you and appointed you to go and bear fruit — fruit that will last. Then the Father will give you whatever you ask in my name.

John 15:15-16

Serving

Do nothing out of selfish ambition or vain conceit, but in humility consider others better than yourselves. Each of you should look not only to your own interests, but also to the interests of others.
Philippians 2:3-4

I was pregnant after only seven months of marriage. My excitement was incredible. I told everyone the good news and I worshipped God with thanksgiving. As time passed, though, I began to dwell on the realities of raising a baby. A dark cloud set in. Soon my thoughts and conversations were cluttered with phrases that went like this: "After the baby is born, I won't be able to…" "get the sleep I need" or "go to the movies with my husband whenever I want" or "spontaneously head for the beach." I had better enjoy my freedom now, I thought, because in a few months I'll have no life.

"You, my brothers, were called to be free. But do not use your freedom to indulge the sinful nature; rather, serve one another in love"(Galatians 5:13). The problem was my definition of freedom and my understanding of its purpose.

As Christians, we have been set free from the law of sin and death (Romans 8:2); set free so that we can serve others. What I was dreading was not a loss of freedom. I just didn't want to have to serve another person, not even my own child. I didn't want to get up for 2 a.m. feedings. I didn't want to have to prepare a diaper bag for every outing. I didn't want to have to turn down opportunities because of my baby. I wanted to be able to do what I wanted, when I wanted.

That is selfishness. And we are called to be the exact opposite — servants. Jesus, our example for life, said in Matthew 20:28 that He "did not come to be served, but to serve." What better way to learn this than to be given a brand new baby who is completely dependent. We are instantly servants; instantly more like Christ.

God, in His infinite wisdom, is the one that created our babies to be so dependent. Look at the other creatures in the world. None of them are as helpless as a newborn human. God knows that our babies will need us, night and day. He made them that way.

God, in His infinite love, also made babies irresistible. I didn't know that I would love holding my baby in the quiet of the night, that I would enjoy showing off my baby while we were out, that I would have fun staying home playing with my baby. Thank You, Lord, for these wonderful rewards.

–MLG

Prayer

Prepare me now, Lord, to care for my baby. Help me to put this baby's interests ahead of my own. I do not want to resent serving my baby; instead, I want to rejoice in the fact that You are using my baby to make me more like Christ, for that is truly my goal. Amen.

For further study ~ John 13:1-17

I Want to Be a Servant

Do I currently avoid opportunities to serve? Why or why not?

_____

_____

_____

_____

Do I need to repent for my attitude about serving this child from God? If so, here is my prayer of repentance:

_____

_____

_____

_____

_____

_____

Besides helping me learn to serve others, how else might this child be used to conform me to the image of Christ?

_____

_____

_____

_____

The King will reply, "I tell you the truth, whatever you did for one of the least of these brothers of mine, you did for me."
~ Matthew 25:40

A Daily Dose of Compassion

The Lord's loving kindnesses indeed never cease,
for his compassions never fail. They are new every
morning; Great is Thy faithfulness.
Lamentations 3:22-23 NASB

Aaaah…My baby's birth. What a sweet and tender moment! For nine months she had been growing in my womb, and now she makes her way down the birth canal, about to burst out into the loving arms of her family. Garbled sounds that have filled her ears become crisp and clear as she enters her new world. Almost out now, she can recognize her mother's voice, a comforting voice throughout the past months, a voice that has often lulled her to sleep, a voice that is now screaming, "PULL IT OUT! JUST PULL IT OUT!"

In Genesis 3:16, God says, "I will greatly increase your pains in childbearing; with pain you will give birth to children." The Bible says it; I believe it. Childbirth is painful. There are many drugs available to help the process, but most women will experience pain either during labor or recovery.

I have not found it to be a glamorous event either. I was not dressed in a pure white gown trimmed in lace with my hair falling softly on my shoulders. I was dressed in a cheap blue smock with a gaping humiliation hole in back, and the only hair on my shoulders was what I had pulled out in frustration. I'll say this: childbirth is beautiful, but it sure ain't pretty!

Usually, I'm excited about having another baby. But every once in a while, the pain looms in front of me. It's like a huge brick wall, and I truly don't think I have the strength to climb it. I don't want to be in that much pain. I just don't think I can do it again.

It is then that I remember the truth in the third chapter of Lamentations. God's loving kindness and compassions are new every morning. When we wake up on the day that our babies will be born, we will have the mercy from God that we need to make it through labor. We don't have that mercy today, because we don't need it today.

This is true in all situations. That's one of the reasons worrying is fruitless. When we are in the midst of a trial, God gives us what we need. God is gracious and merciful (Nehemiah 9:31). When we worry about the future, though, we are imagining the situation without the benefits of God's mercy for that day — we are viewing it with the strength we have today, not with the strength that we will have when that day arrives.

Let's remember that our God is "full of compassion and mercy"(James 5:11). We can count on His kindness to help us through every situation.

–MLG

Prayer

God, I know I don't need to worry because You are a kind and compassionate God. Please help me to remember that You are with me today, and you will be with me tomorrow, no matter what I face. I want to live my life knowing that I am in the hands of a loving Father. Amen.

For further study ~ Psalm 28

My God Is Compassionate and Kind

When I picture God, what do I see?

_____

_____

_____

_____

_____

_____

How does this image affect the way I view childbirth? How does this image affect the way I view the future?

_____

_____

_____

_____

What steps can I take today to renew my mind and face the future with confidence as the daughter of the Almighty and Compassionate Father?

_____

_____

_____

_____

*Let us then approach the throne of grace
with confidence, so that we may receive mercy
and find grace to help us in our time of need.
~ Hebrews 4:16*

When We Are Wrong

Therefore confess your sins to each other and pray for each other so that you may be healed.
James 5:16

It has been said that it is easier to build children than to repair adults. Yes, we want to do it the right way from the beginning so they will not be struggling with basic biblical principles when they are grown. We want them to have the security of our love and God's love throughout their lives. We're going to encourage them. We're going to discipline them in love. We're going to be supportive. We're going to have daily devotions with them. We're going to have regular times of family worship. We're going to evangelize and serve the poor together.

We're going to fail.

We will not be able to always keep these standards. We are sinners, and we will not be perfect. What do we do then? Will our children be permanently scarred because of our failures?

The best thing we can do when we mess up as parents is to confess our sin. Not just to the Lord, but also to our children. The benefits of this are numerous.

It is biblical. If we lie to our children, we need to ask their forgiveness.

It is cleansing. We are able to have relationships with our children with nothing lingering between us.

It is humbling. Asking our children to forgive us is an excellent reminder of our own sinfulness.

It is setting a good pattern for the family. Our children will learn from our example.

It is evangelistic. As we openly confess our sins and obvious need for the Savior, our children will more readily identify their own sin and their personal need for Christ.

What age should our children be when we start asking their forgiveness?

It is never too early. A child's comprehension vocabulary exceeds her speaking vocabulary. She will understand what we say much earlier than we might think. It is good practice for us to begin with the first time we make a mistake so that forgiveness becomes a habit in our lives, and the lives of our children.

Our babies are still in our wombs, so in essence we have a clean parenting slate in front of us. We may not be able to meet the goals set forth above, but there is one we can definitely achieve: we can ask our children's forgiveness when we fail. It's never too early, and it's never too late.

–MLG

Prayer

Lord, this sounds so simple on paper, but so difficult to do. I want to love my child and respect her enough to ask her forgiveness when I'm wrong. She is not a doll for me to treat as I want, but she is a human being with feelings. Please help me to remember that. Amen.

For further study ~ Colossians 3:12-17

When I Am Wrong

Do I confess my sins to the Lord? Why or why not?

_____

_____

_____

_____

Do I ask people to forgive me when I do something wrong? Why or why not?

_____

_____

_____

_____

Do I appreciate when someone asks my forgiveness? How does it affect our relationship?

_____

_____

_____

_____

Do to others as you would have them do to you.
~ Luke 6:31

According to His Kindness

I will tell of the kindnesses of the Lord, the deeds for which he is to be praised, according to all the Lord has done for us — yes, the many good things he has done for the house of Israel, according to his compassion and many kindnesses.
Isaiah 63:7

"The baby can hear what I say? Wow!"

I was overjoyed that my "relationship" with my child was officially beginning. I knew I had been playing a vital role in the physical development, but now, in the middle of my second trimester, my baby's personality was beginning to form. I could communicate with him. What would I tell him? What would I say? Should I sing or tell my life story? Maybe I should begin with the Bible. Yes, I will tell my baby about his Creator! Some of the first words my baby hears can be the wisdom from God.

Whenever we sing praises to God, our babies are exposed to worship. Whenever we read aloud from the Bible, they are hearing the Word of God. Our babies can be a part of family devotions! What a testimony for our children to one day be able to say, "From as long as I can remember I knew about God."

How much of this will our babies understand? Scientists can give us their opinion but only God really knows. What we do know is that God is a kind God. He enables us to speak the truth to our children before any ungodly influence can reach their little ears. We can be the first to preach the gospel to them. It is not too soon to tell these tiny, new lives about the Creator of the universe and the Creator of life itself.

–MK

Prayer

Lord God, what a privilege to be the first to introduce my child to You. Help me to remember many stories of Your kindness so I may tell them to my little baby and be a godly influence from the beginning. Amen.

For further study ~ Titus 3:4-8

According to His Kindness

Here are some ways that I can introduce my baby to God:

_____

_____

_____

_____

_____

This is my first memory of God:

_____

_____

_____

_____

God has shown me His kindness in this circumstance:

_____

_____

_____

_____

I led them with cords of human kindness,
with ties of love; I lifted the yoke from
their neck and bent down to feed them.
~ Hosea 11:4

Clothed in Christ

Therefore, as God's chosen people, holy and dearly loved, clothe yourselves with compassion, kindness, humility, gentleness and patience. Bear with each other and forgive whatever grievances you may have against one another. Forgive as the Lord forgave you. And over all these virtues put on love, which binds them all together in perfect unity.
Colossians 3:12-14

I stood in front of the closet, trying to decide what to wear. My "skinny" clothes were gone — packed away with the high hopes that they would one day be needed again. My wardrobe was cut in half, but what was left "doubled in size." There was nothing there that I wanted to wear.

The good news is, God doesn't look at the clothes we wear. He looks at how we clothe our hearts. When was the last time we put on compassion? Do we daily adorn ourselves with kindness? Do we reach for humility as our undergarment so that gentleness and patience can be the main attraction?

Colossians 3:13 challenges us to "bear with each other and forgive whatever grievances you may have against one another." It is much easier to walk in forgiveness if we've chosen the right clothes for the journey. Consider the example of Jesus. He was clothed in compassion, kindness, humility, gentleness and patience as He was nailed to the cross.

Even though Jesus set the perfect example, we often fall short. We sometimes choose harshness instead of gentleness and kindness. At times we think we are better than others instead of wearing humility. We may cloak our hearts in anger instead of responding in patience and compassion. How can we clothe ourselves in godly virtues instead of reaching for what comes easiest?

Galatians 2:20 says, "I have been crucified with Christ and I no longer live, but Christ lives in me. The life I live in the body, I live by faith in the Son of God, who loved me and gave himself for me." It is only by faith in Christ that we can clothe ourselves in these godly virtues. He is the One who has provided our spiritual clothing and He is the One who helps us make the right choices.

We may have to change several times throughout the day as we realize we've put on the wrong garments. The door to the closet is always open. No matter what we put on, we are the ones who are making the choices. Let's not walk away from our prayer closet unless we are fully dressed as God's chosen people.

–MK

Prayer

Jesus, You are the perfect example. You have given me everything I need to follow You, yet so often I fall short, and so do those around me. Help me to put on Your compassion, to accent what I wear with kindness and gentleness. In humility and patience help me to bear with others and walk in forgiveness. Amen.

For further study ~ 2 Peter 1:3-11

Am I Clothed in Christ?

Which virtues do I avoid wearing?

_____

_____

_____

_____

When I face the circumstances of my day, what can I do to remind myself to put on godly virtues?

_____

_____

_____

_____

This is how I am affected when I read and meditate on Galatians 2:20:

_____

_____

_____

_____

_____

*Be kind and compassionate
to one another, forgiving each other,
just as in Christ God forgave you.
~ Ephesians 4:32*

Motivated by Grace

But in your great mercy you did not put an end to them or abandon them, for you are a gracious and merciful God.
Nehemiah 9:31

I peeked in the shower to inspect the work that had been done. The tub sparkled, but the shower doors were covered in soap scum and mold was still growing above the faucet. Could anything ever be done right?

I like my house clean, yet I had been ordered by my midwife to rest. So I entrusted the cleaning to my husband and children. They were serving me heroically, but in my heart it was never good enough. Most of the work was not up to my standards. When I asked him about the incomplete job, my husband replied, "I worked so hard on getting the tub clean that I didn't even think about the rest of the shower."

The choice was now mine. I could vent all my frustrations on my already over-worked husband, or I could respond to him as I would want God to respond to me when I fall short. I walked away with my mouth closed, and went to God with my frustrated heart.

My husband did not sin when he only cleaned half the tub; he just didn't do it the way I wanted it done. How should we treat others when they fall short of our expectations? Or what if they sin against us? Do we charge them and hold it against them until they make it right? Do these actions motivate others in grace?

How does God treat us when we fall short of His standard? 2 Corinthians 5:19 says, "God was reconciling the world to himself in Christ, not counting men's sins against them." God knows we fall short, yet day after day He continues to respond to us with grace and mercy. He is always forgiving, kind, compassionate and slow to anger. Do we extend that same grace to others?

—MK

Prayer

Oh, Lord, I fall short so often and so do those around me. Help me to respond to them as You respond to me, in love and grace. Let me be motivated by Your example and treat others as You treat me. Amen.

For further study ~ 2 Corinthians 5:14-21

God's Grace Through Me

How have I had to change my standards because of this pregnancy?

_____

_____

_____

_____

_____

_____

Have I felt God's grace for me in this? In what way?

_____

_____

_____

_____

_____

How can I motivate others with grace?

_____

_____

_____

_____

_____

Dear friends, since God so loved us,
we also ought to love one another.
~1 John 4:11

Named by God

But rejoice that your names are written in heaven.
Luke 10:20

Ashley, Jessica or Sarah.

Michael, Joshua or Matthew.

There are so many names to choose from! Yet so few my husband and I agree on. How will I ever choose a name for this baby?

Are names really that important? Yes! They give people their identities. They distinguish us from others. They have the potential to be admired, liked or disliked. The names we choose for our children will be a part of them for the rest of their lives.

Names are important to God. He determines the number of the stars and calls them each by name (Psalm 147:4). God has plans for our children; certainly He has names for them as well. Have we stopped to ask God what we should name our babies?

The meaning of a name is significant. Certainly we would not want to name a boy "Nabal," which means "fool" (1 Samuel 25:25). "Michael" is an inspiring name — it means "who is like the Lord." What Christian parents wouldn't want their son to be like the Lord? It is no surprise that Michael has been one of the most popular names in the U.S. for over fifty years.

You may have known since you were a child what you wanted to name all of your children. Or, you may have the baby in your arms and still not know what to name her. If God numbers our hairs (Luke 12:7), and provides for our lives (Matthew 6:25-32), then surely He knows our babies' names.

As we seek God, we can rejoice that our own names are written in heaven and trust Him to reveal the names for our babies.

—MK

Prayer

Thank You, Father, that You care about every detail of my life. You know my baby's name. I ask You to reveal that special name to me. More importantly, I want my child to bring glory to Your Name. Amen.

For further study ~ John 10:1-18

Named by God

My process for choosing my baby's name included:

_____

_____

_____

Jesus is my Shepherd and knows me by name. How does this perspective affect the naming of my baby?

_____

_____

_____

_____

These are the names selected for my baby and their meanings.

Boy: _____

_____

Girl: _____

_____

But the angel said to him:
"Do not be afraid, Zechariah; your prayer has
been heard. Your wife Elizabeth will bear you a
son, and you are to give him the name John."
~ Luke 1:13

Belt of Truth

Stand firm then, with the belt of truth buckled around your waist.
Ephesians 6:14

I love belts. They accent what I wear, make my waist look thin, and can even hold up my pants. Now that I am pregnant, belts are a thing of the past. I look at my rack of belts and long to be able to fit one around my bulging belly. It is a joke to see how much the gap between the buckle and the end of the belt grows as each month goes by. Belts are no longer flattering. The only belts that are included in maternity clothes are the little ties on the back — the ones that keep the dresses from looking too huge before I actually need every bit of that tent in the last month!

In His kindness, God has provided a belt I can wear throughout pregnancy that is always flattering. It doesn't remind me how far my skin is stretching or which favorite clothes no longer fit. It is a belt the Bible tells me to buckle around my waist — one size fits all! It is the belt of truth.

Ephesians 6 describes the spiritual armor that God gives us so that we can "take [our] stand against the devil's schemes" (verse 11) and when the day of evil comes, we can "stand [our] ground" (verse 13). The belt of truth is the first piece of this armor. It protects the loins and holds much of the armor together.

In His kindness, God has provided this protection so that we will not be deceived. There are many things in this world that are not true. Things that subtly distract us and try to get us off the straight and narrow path to God.

Often, we may be subtly deceived because "everyone else is doing it." Or we may be tempted to tell a "white lie" or be less than accurate on our tax forms. But as Christians our standard is not what everyone else is doing — our standard is Jesus.

In John 14:6, Jesus answered, "I am the way and the truth and the life. No one comes to the Father except through me."

The truth is centrally located between "the way" and "the life" in this passage. It is central to our walk with Jesus because He is the Truth and He is the only way to God! The Bible gives us the truth about Jesus, ourselves and what God desires for our lives. Everything we do should be done according to the truth of God's Word. When we put on His protective armor we can walk in the world and stand firmly for the truth.

–MK

Prayer

Jesus, You give me strength and equip me in Your truth. Open my eyes to where deception is hindering my growth. Show me the way to implement the Word, so I may walk in Your truth and have freedom in this life. Amen.

For further study ~ Ephesians 6:10-18

Putting on the Truth

This is an area where I need to be better equipped in God's truth:

_____

_____

_____

_____

This is my prayer asking God to illuminate areas where I am blinded:

_____

_____

_____

_____

_____

Here is a situation where the truth has set me free:

_____

_____

_____

_____

Then you will know the truth,
and the truth will set you free.
~ John 8:32

Faithfulness

*This is to my Father's glory, that you bear
much fruit, showing yourselves to be my disciples.*
—John 15:8

Glorifying the Lord

Come and listen, all you who fear God;
let me tell you what he has done for me.
Psalm 66:16

Jesus was walking to Jerusalem. On the way, ten men with leprosy stood beside the road, crying out to Jesus to have pity on them. He healed them all, but the Scripture says that only one of them "came back, praising God in a loud voice" (Luke 17:15). When Jesus saw this, He asked, "Where are the other nine?"

God has done a tremendous miracle in our lives by placing a child in each of our wombs. But what has been our response? Are we with the nine—excited about our gift, but too busy to give glory to the Giver? Sure, we're thankful, but have we joined with the faithful one who came back and praised God in a loud voice?

Psalm 29:2 says that we are to "ascribe to the Lord the glory due his name." Not now, Lord. We're sick. We're tired. We're swollen. We're busy. We're pregnant. Certainly God doesn't expect us to "declare his glory among the nations, his marvelous deeds among all peoples"(Psalm 96:3)?

I've looked, but there's just no pregnancy loophole in this verse. The good news is that God made it easy for us during this challenging time. Look at your life recently. Think of all the people who have taken an interest in you, just because you're pregnant. Neighbors, co-workers, relatives, people at the grocery store—many people that now go out of their way to speak to you. Sometimes they bring gloomy predictions and unwanted advice, but that's even more reason to reach out to them with the truth of God's Word. In Mark 16:15, Jesus says to "Go into all the world and preach the good news to all creation." We have it easy—the world is coming to us!

What do we do now? How do we take advantage of the opportunities that the Lord is giving us during pregnancy? 1 Peter 4:11 sets the standard: "If anyone speaks, he should do it as one speaking the very words of God. If anyone serves, he should do it with the strength God provides, so that in all things God may be praised through Jesus Christ." Our assignment is to cry out for God's strength and look for ways to praise Him.

How about birth announcements? Why elevate cuteness above the opportunity to publicly proclaim that our babies are gifts from the Lord? The same is true with thank-you notes for shower gifts. We can make these testimonies of God's goodness, too.

Conversations are often an excellent occasion to bring glory to God. Here are some examples that may come your way:

1. Comment: "You're pregnant? Congratulations!"

Response: "Thanks. I am thrilled that God is giving me a baby."

2. Comment: "When are you due?"

Response: "I'm due in August. I know it'll be a long, hot summer, but I'm just glad God has given me this baby."

3. Comment: "Wow, your life is about to change!"

Response: "I'm sure it is. The Bible says this baby is a blessing from God."

4. Comment: "Enjoy them while they're young, because once they get to be teenagers…forget it!"

Response: "You know, I'm planning on using the Bible as my guide for raising this child, so I have a lot of hope for the future."

Instead of seeing this season of life as a time that we are "out of commission," let's open our eyes to the unique opportunities we have to fulfill the Great Commission.

–MLG

Prayer

Father, I am so thankful You have placed this child in my womb. I want to be like the faithful leper and praise You not only in my own heart, but also with a loud voice. This pregnancy gives me many opportunities to reach out to others. Please give me the words to say as I seek to glorify You in all that I do.

For further study ~ Colossians 4:2-6

I Want to Glorify the Lord

Who are the people that I now have the opportunity to reach out to as a result of my pregnancy?

_____

_____

_____

What are the questions or comments that I regularly receive from others?

_____

_____

_____

What responses can I give that will bring glory to God?

_____

_____

_____

But the Lord stood at my side and
gave me strength, so that through me the
message might be fully proclaimed and
all the Gentiles might hear it.
~ 2 Timothy 4:17

Prayer

*So now I give him to the Lord. For his
whole life he will be given over to the Lord.*
1 Samuel 1:28

Hannah was an excellent woman—a woman of courage, a woman of conviction, a woman of love, a woman of faith…a woman I wouldn't want to trade places with! I am glad that God has not asked me to do what Hannah did: to give birth to a son and then, after he is weaned, take him up to the temple and leave him there to be raised by the priest. I am thrilled that I will probably get to spend lots of time with my child, talking with him, comforting him, and playing with him. My calling as a mother is different than Hannah's, but does that mean I can just read her story with a sigh of relief and move on?

No, 2 Timothy 3:16 says that "all Scripture is God-breathed and is useful for teaching, rebuking, correcting and training in righteousness." So what can we learn from Hannah? One thing we can see is the importance of following her example and giving our own babies to the Lord.

But wait a minute. Our babies have not even been born yet. How can we give them to the Lord?

We give them to the Lord through prayer. Praying for our babies demonstrates that we know they belong to Him. Job 41:11 quotes the Lord as saying, "Everything under heaven belongs to me." By turning to the Lord and asking for Him to keep our babies healthy, to bless them, to protect them, to nourish them, we are acknowledging that they belong to Him and we can not do these things without the Lord's help.

Praying for our babies is also a testimony that we know the Lord is ultimately in charge of their lives. Sure, we want to be responsible parents and do our best. But Proverbs 20:24 tells us that the Lord directs people's steps, and that includes the steps of our babies.

We are mothers. From the minute God placed our babies within us, we became mothers. Our bodies began to change, our emotions began to change, and our perspectives began to change. Let's not wait until we have our babies in our arms to begin praying. It's never too early to pray! Let's daily cry out to the Lord, knowing that He sees our babies even now.

–MLG

Prayer

Lord, I want to be a faithful mother even from the beginning. I also want to be a faithful mother to the end, praying for my child all the days of my life. I give my baby to You, and I want to daily turn to You to protect, nourish, and direct my child's life. Amen.

For further study ~ Psalm 16

Prayers for My Child

To my child,

I have prayed for you according to these examples from Scripture. I make a commitment on this day_____ to faithfully pray these things for you throughout your life.

I love you,

Mom

I pray, my child, that "the God of our Lord Jesus Christ, the Father of glory, may give to you a spirit of wisdom and of revelation in the knowledge of Him. I pray that the eyes of your heart may be enlightened, so that you will know what is the hope of His calling, what are the riches of the glory of His inheritance in the saints, and what is the surpassing greatness of His power toward us who believe."

~Ephesians 1:17-19 NASB

My child, I "have not ceased to pray for you and to ask that you may be filled with the knowledge of His will in all spiritual wisdom and understanding, so that you will walk in a manner worthy of the Lord, to please Him in all respects, bearing fruit in every good work and increasing in the knowledge of God; strengthened with all power, according to His glorious might."

~Colossians 1:9-11 NASB

Here is a prayer for you in my own words:

_____

_____

_____

_____

_____

_____

Pray continually.
~1 Thessalonians 5:17

A Marked Woman

*And it will be like a sign on your hand and
a symbol on your forehead that the Lord brought us
out of Egypt with his mighty hand.*
Exodus 13:16

I glanced at the mirror before stepping in the shower. It had happened. Pink streaks ran across my expanding belly. They had also organized around my now 38C breasts. Stretching down the outside of my thighs, blue spider veins seemed to pop out upon inspection. I was a marked woman! I knew I would bear these signs of childbirth 'til my dying day. I was a baby factory with stress cracks appearing around my edges.

After the exile to Babylon, Jews began the literal practice of writing Scripture texts on strips of parchment. They placed them in small leather boxes and strapped them to their foreheads and left arms. The Jews did this to remind them of God's faithfulness for delivering them out of Egypt. The boxes were called "phylacteries."

Stretch marks and spider veins are tied to our bodies in a similar way. Our bodies will be forever branded with these marks. They will be our phylacteries— a constant reminder of God's faithfulness as He brought us through the beautiful, painful, miraculous process of birth. God's mighty hand will lead us through, as He led the children of Israel through the Red Sea.

When we look at these marks and are tempted to despair, we see them as reminders, but not only for us. If our children catch glimpses of them, we can use the opportunity to tell them of God's faithfulness. Whatever marks we bear will be a constant reminder of the tremendous blessings God has given us.

—MK

Prayer

Lord, You are a faithful God extending Your mercy to all generations. Help me to accept the changes in my body as a sign of Your faithfulness, and to tell of Your goodness to the next generation. As You have marked my body, mark my mind and heart with Your faithfulness.

For further study ~ Proverbs 3:1-8

I Am a Marked Woman

This is how I have been marked by God's faithfulness during my pregnancy:

_____

_____

_____

_____

I view these marks on my body from pregnancy as:

_____

_____

To my precious child, here is a story from my pregnancy that I want to pass on to you:

_____

_____

_____

_____

_____

_____

_____

_____

_____

God, who has called you into fellowship with his Son Jesus Christ our Lord, is faithful.
~1 Corinthians 1:9

Let Me Tell You
What the Lord Has Done

*Only be careful, and watch yourselves closely so that
you do not forget the things your eyes have seen or let them
slip from your heart as long as you live. Teach them to
your children and to their children after them.*
Deuteronomy 4:9

Having a baby is about more than bonnets and booties, bottles and blankets. Having a baby is also about health insurance and investments, life insurance and inheritances.

We want to make wise decisions so our babies' financial needs are met now and in the future. Some may even have priceless heirlooms set aside as part of their children's inheritance. All of these are good, but the most valuable thing we can pass on to our children is a legacy of faith.

Children love to hear stories from the Bible about our powerful God. They also love to hear true stories about people they know. By taking advantage of these natural interests, we can transform their images of God from One who did miracles and led His people a long time ago to the God of today, the One who still leads His people and does miracles…in our own families.

We have the audience: our children. We have the motive: to build our children's faith. Now we can focus on us: the storytellers. Deuteronomy 4:9 tells us to be careful and watch that we don't forget what we've seen. What a timely warning for today! Our lives are filled with appointments and activities. We rush through our days, without taking the time to contemplate on all that has happened. We can barely remember what happened last week, so how can we expect to remember what the Lord did for us two years ago, and then find the time to tell our children about it?

The best way to combat this tendency to "let them slip from our heart" is to write down examples of God's faithfulness in our lives. This will not only provide the details to jolt our memories, it will also give us a permanent record that we can hand down to our children. That's what makes a book like this a priceless treasure, both for us and for the generations to come.

The Lord is moving in our lives everyday. Sometimes we see His hand in a dramatic way, such as a physical healing. Sometimes it is His still, small voice that gently directs us to give a lonely friend a call. Both of these are testimonies of God's faithfulness in our lives. These are the stories we need to be telling our children regularly to build their faith and confidence that the Lord will do the same in their lives.

While I was in the middle of writing this book, a friend from church offered to babysit my children one day so that I could devote more time to writing. She had a dream that she had offered to do this for me, and when she awoke, she knew it was the Lord prompting her. I said yes to her generous offer and excitedly told my children the news:

"Guess what? Miss Ann had a dream that she asked me if you could spend the day at her house so I could get some writing done. When she woke up, she knew the dream was from God, and she would like to have you over on Wednesday."

My children were grinning as I continued. "Can you believe that? God loves me so much, and loves you so much, that He talked to Miss Ann in a dream and told her to help us out. Isn't that amazing?"

Yes, it is amazing, and that's what we need to pass on to our children: the amazing stories of God's faithfulness, power and love.

–MLG

Prayer

Lord, You have done amazing things in my life and in the lives of people I know. I can now look back on situations that I didn't understand at the time and see Your sovereign hand leading me and protecting me. All of these stories are precious treasures that I want to give to my child. Help me to not let them "slip from my heart." Amen.

For further study ~ Deuteronomy 6:20-25

A Legacy of God's Faithfulness

One of the most important stories for me to share with my child is when I made Jesus Lord of my life. Here are the details surrounding my conversion:

_____

_____

_____

_____

Here's a story about a trial I faced, and how the Lord led me through it:

_____

_____

_____

Here's a story about how God used Scripture to change my life in a dramatic way:

_____

_____

_____

Guard the good deposit that was
entrusted to you — guard it with the help
of the Holy Spirit who lives in us.
~2 Timothy 1:14

Wisdom for Mothers

He tends his flock like a shepherd: He gathers
the lambs in his arms and carries them close to his heart;
he gently leads those that have young.
Isaiah 40:11

"Now don't you worry. You've still got plenty of time before that baby is ready to come out," the nurse assured me.

"No, I really think it's time," I insisted.

"We just checked you a little while ago and I even called your doctor. He'll be here in about two hours." The nurse turned to walk out the door.

Suddenly a deep, guttural voice rose from within me and I screamed, "THE BABY'S COMING NOW!"

The delivery room was instantly filled with the clanking sound of metal tools and carts being wheeled into place. Someone grabbed a doctor from the hallway. She snapped on her gloves and…plop…caught my baby.

The staff at that hospital knew a lot more about childbirth than me. They had taken more courses, studied more books, and assisted in more deliveries. I had something, though, that they didn't. I had the "Mommy Advantage."

This is true for each of us, not just in the delivery room, but for the rest of our children's lives—we will have the advantage. Soon after we bring our babies home from the hospitals, we can recognize a hungry cry from a hurt cry. We are mommies. One day we will be able to just look into our children's eyes and tell that they're sick. We are mommies. There will be a time when we only have to hear our children's voices to know that something is wrong. We are mommies.

Where does this insight come from? And where can we get more? Proverbs 2:6 says, "For the Lord gives wisdom, and from his mouth come knowledge and understanding." Does that mean that all we need to do is read the Bible and pray? Those are two powerful tools, but Proverbs also says that "wisdom is found in those who take advice" (Proverbs 13:10).

Here are two questions to consider before seeking advice. The first is, Why am I asking this person? For instance, I may see someone with respectful and friendly children and ask for some child rearing tips. That is seeing the fruit and wanting to learn how it got there.

The second question is, What is this person's foundation for life? As Christians, our foundations for life are Jesus Christ and the Bible. Any advice we receive needs to be weighed against Scripture. For example, if the mother of the friendly and respectful children says the key to her success is that she plays New Age music throughout her home and has a crystal hanging in every room, I would not apply that advice in my home because it does not line up with Scripture. "See to it that no one takes you captive through hollow and deceptive philosophy, which depends on human tradition and the basic principles of this world rather than on Christ" (Colossians 2:8).

Our children belong to God, and He will give us the wisdom to lead them as we seek Him and seek godly counsel. Do not be intimidated by professionals or anyone else. Yes, we need their help, we need their knowledge and we need their experience. But with the Lord's help, we are able to receive their advice, compare it to Scripture, pray, and make the best decisions. We can do this, and we will do this, because we have the Mommy Advantage.

–MLG

Prayer

Lord, I don't want to be arrogant, but I also know that no one else on earth, besides my husband, will love this child like I do. I am looking to You to give me wisdom in raising my child. I want to be teachable, and yet, I want to be strong in the confidence that You have given me this child and You will lead me. Amen.

For further study ~ Proverbs 4

Wisdom for Me

To whom do I turn for advice? Am I receiving godly counsel?

_____

_____

_____

How did I choose my obstetrician? How will I choose my pediatrician? Do they have the same foundation for life that I do? Do they place a high value on human life and believe that my child was made in the image of the Lord (Genesis 1:27)?

_____

_____

_____

Am I seeking the Lord's counsel throughout the day? Am I confidently looking to Him to guide my decisions? Why, or why not?

_____

_____

_____

If any of you lacks wisdom, he should ask
God, who gives generously to all without
finding fault, and it will be given to him.
~ James 1:5

Milk or Solid Food?

But solid food is for the mature, who by constant use have trained themselves to distinguish good from evil.
Hebrews 5:14

Breast-fed or bottle-fed? Whatever form we choose, babies from all countries and all economic backgrounds need the same thing: milk.

The same is true for us as Christians. When we first make a commitment to the Lord, we are like babies. Much of the teachings in the Bible are new to us, and we take small steps as we begin our lives in Christ. What we need during this time is spiritual milk.

"Like newborn babies, crave pure spiritual milk, so that by it you may grow up in your salvation, now that you have tasted that the Lord is good" (1 Peter 2:2-3). That is the purpose of milk—to help us grow. Just as a baby matures and is eventually ready for solid food, we are to grow in the Lord and mature. But does this process happen naturally to every Christian?

Scripture shows us that it does not. In 1 Corinthians chapter 3, Paul gives a word of correction to the church in Corinth. Though they had been Christians for some time, Paul says that they were still "infants in Christ." What caused Paul to come to this conclusion? "I gave you milk, not solid food, for you were not yet ready for it. Indeed, you are still not ready. You are still worldly" (1 Corinthians 3:2-3).

Worldliness is in direct opposition to Christlikeness. Life can be placed on a continuum, with worldliness on one end and Christlikeness on the other. Before we make a commitment to Christ, we are completely worldly, using our own distorted standards to determine what is right and wrong. Once we become a Christian, though, we begin moving forward, becoming more like Christ every step of the way. But how do we keep moving along this continuum, away from worldliness and toward Christ?

Hebrews 5:14 says that it is the "constant use" of biblical teachings that causes us to become less worldly and able to "distinguish good from evil." It is not enough to hear good teachings and read the Bible, we must be using what we've learned and apply it to our lives if we want to grow up in the Lord.

Because God is our Father, we can be free from the pressure to be instantly perfect. No parent expects his newborn to get up and run around the block. In the same way, God expects His children to be faithfully growing in Him day by day.

When evaluating our growth, it is important that we not compare ourselves to anyone else. We should be inspired by more mature Christians, but our standard is to be the Word of God. We are to look at our own lives and determine if we are actively obeying the Scriptures in faith—moving from spiritual milk to solid food.

Have we grown comfortable sitting on a pew on Sunday mornings, thinking that we're growing in the Lord? Do we think that because we read our Bibles and pray that we are living godly lives and becoming more like Christ? Knowledge does not change us. It is the application of knowledge that leads to true change.

–MLG

Prayer

Lord, I don't want to stagnate in my walk with You. I know it is Your desire that I not remain an infant in Christ my whole life, but that I faithfully apply Your Word and mature into all that You have for me. Amen.

For further study ~ Matthew 7:24-27

Am I Growing in the Lord?

Is the Bible the standard for my life? In what ways is this evident?

_____

_____

_____

As I look back over the past year, in what areas have I turned from my old ways and become more like Christ?

_____

_____

_____

Do I expect too much from myself, not receiving the grace from God to grow one step at a time? In what areas do I try to achieve my own goals, instead of God's?

_____

_____

_____

Do not merely listen to the word, and
so deceive yourselves. Do what it says.
~ James 1:22

All I Have

All these people gave their gifts out of their wealth; but she out of her poverty put in all she had to live on.
Luke 21:4

A group of 18- to 25-year-olds, full of the Lord and full of His strength, came to help our new church. They sowed random acts of kindness to show the love of God and to make our church's presence known in the community. There were service projects, free car washes, soda and orange juice giveaways, one-on-one witnessing, and a free family festival. I participated fully with these young people, known as the "E-Team" (Evangelism Team). I experienced all of the fun and all of the work.

A year later, when the E-Team came again, my situation was different. I was pregnant, with a mid-wife's orders to take it easy. I was supposed to be resting, so how could I wash cars, paint and clean for a local ministry, and stand on a street corner giving away soda? My husband, my pastor and many of the E-Teamers insisted that I stay home. They used my home for meals and a meeting place so I saw them at the end of each day when they returned full of excitement. I rejoiced in what God was doing through them, but a part of me was sad because I was not able to do it with them.

The E-Teamers were youthful and strong, giving their all out of the abundance of their energies. I, on the other hand, was exhausted after only wiping the kitchen counter. I felt like I was lying around doing nothing; I wanted to do so much more.

The story of the widow's offering in Luke 21 offers encouragement for situations like mine. The widow did her part, which was valuable in the sight of the Lord. In the same way, I was doing my part, which was also valuable in His sight. My part happened to be equivalent to about two very small, copper coins (Luke 21:2). But at that time, it was all I could give.

Our season of life changes when we have children. We are about to give birth to little lives that need to be loved and discipled day after day. It starts with the dirty diapers and 2 a.m. feedings. Then it grows into questions like: "Where do butterflies come from?" And progresses to questions like: "What is heaven, and will I go there?" This is the time to focus our energy at home. God will give us opportunities to share our faith and serve others, but it's okay if it isn't the same method that it used to be. God is faithful to use us where we are.

These days will not last forever; they will fly by. Before we realize where the time went, our children will be the ones out there doing service projects—full of energy and full of the presence of the Lord, giving all they have to serve God.

–MK

Prayer

Lord, please give me the strength to rest in You and to not be distracted by what You are doing in others. Change my heart so I may be content, and give me a passion so I may make the most of this season of life.

For further study ~ Ecclesiastes 3:1-14

All I Have

Here is a list of what I have had to give up because I am pregnant:

_____

_____

_____

_____

_____

These are my feelings about having to give up things I enjoy doing for the Lord:

_____

_____

_____

_____

This is what I am able to give to God in this season of life:

_____

_____

_____

_____

*Whoever obeys his command will come
to no harm, and the wise heart will know
the proper time and procedure.
~ Ecclesiastes 8:5*

A Time to Plant

*So neither he who plants nor he who waters is anything,
but only God, who makes things grow. The man who plants
and the man who waters have one purpose, and each will be
rewarded according to his own labor.*

1 Corinthians 3:7-8

When you plant a seed there are many factors involved in its growth. You must cover it, water it, nourish it, and make sure it gets the right amount of sun. Then the miracle takes place. The seed begins to open and grow as God created it to do. A tiny, green shoot appears above the soil and a plant sprouts forth. One day that plant will flower and bear fruit. A strong, sturdy plant will bloom year after year, producing usefulness, beauty and joy.

God has planted a seed in each of our wombs. Soon, that little sprout will emerge, tiny and vulnerable, totally dependent upon us, the caretakers. From the beginning, that sprout will bring us joy. If we nurture this joy with the proper diligence, we will harvest a sturdy, useful and beautiful adult, grounded in God and rooted in His Word.

Ministries, jobs and possessions should not come before family. If we are pouring ourselves into a job so that we can have the money we want, but our children don't know the Lord, then our priorities need adjusting. If we bring a new person to church each week through our bold evangelism but our children are disrespectful, disobedient and without correction, then we need to re-evaluate our choices. If our children see us as a maid instead of a mommy then we need to check our motives for cleanliness. Are we willing to lay aside other activities to ensure that our seeds from God are getting the care they need?

Sometimes we may miss sermons because our babies need extra attention. God is aware of that. When the babies are grown and gone, there will be plenty of time for seminars, ministry to the poor, evangelism, and housekeeping. The seeds God has planted in our families need to be our first fruits. Exodus 23:19 tells us to "bring the best of the firstfruits of your soil to the house of the Lord your God." Out of the fruit of the family flows ministry.

God may have you continue a ministry or keep your job after the baby is born. If that is God's will for your life, you will have the grace to maintain His priorities. However, don't feel left behind if you have to serve in different ways for a season so that you can have the time to nurture your little sprout from God. He will still use you, just in different capacities. We need to continually check our hearts to make sure that our husbands and children are being presented as our first fruits to God.

Seed time and harvest take a lot of hard work. God knows how much work it takes to raise a crop of children. If we look to Him for help, and are diligent with what God has given us, then our whole family will be rewarded with the fruit of our labor.

–MK

Prayer

Father, You are Lord of the harvest. I present to You the first fruits of my life: my husband and child. Please help me to reprioritize my life to welcome our new addition with the proper ingredients, so my heart and actions are right in Your eyes.

For further study ~ 2 Corinthians 9:6-15

Committing My First Fruits to God

How can I establish biblical priorities while balancing my family and other activities?

_____

_____

_____

What do I need to do, or do without, so I may best nurture the godly growth of my baby?

_____

_____

_____

_____

In what ways do I think God may use me after my baby is born?

_____

_____

_____

_____

Peacemakers who sow in peace
raise a harvest of righteousness.
~ James 3:18

Gentleness

But the wisdom that comes from heaven is first of all pure;
then peace-loving, considerate, submissive, full of mercy
and good fruit, impartial and sincere.

James 3:17

Standing Before the Throne

After this I looked and there before me was a great multitude that no one could count, from every nation, tribe, people and language, standing before the throne and in front of the Lamb.
Revelation 7:9

I walked through the front door and was greeted by a hearty "Surprise!" My friends from two churches had gathered together to "shower" my baby and me. I had recently left a traditional church and begun attending a non-denominational one. I still had friends at both and nobody allowed doctrinal differences to keep them from coming to honor me and celebrate the upcoming birth of my baby.

When we get together with family or friends from other churches, are we able to gather in unity, based on the belief that Jesus is the only way to heaven? Can we set aside our differences without compromising our doctrinal beliefs? When we discuss doctrinal differences are we making "every effort to keep the unity of the Spirit through the bond of peace?" (Ephesians 4:3).

If we share our hearts in gentleness and humility, it would be difficult to get into a shouting match. When godly people discuss godly topics in an ungodly way, Jesus is not glorified. Unbelievers who see this type of exchange between Christians will be left with a poor example of Christ. There are times when we need to just agree to disagree and let the arguing stop.

Consider that one day we will stand before the throne of God with people who think differently about God than we do. At that time the differences won't seem so big. We won't feel the urge to make sure others know that our way is right and their way is wrong.

Much of our Christian walk is black and white; however, there are areas that are gray. In our personal relationship with Jesus Christ, He deals with each of us individually and leads us through those gray areas. We can celebrate diversity among Christians without compromising the standards of the Bible. We can interact with humility and gentleness, accepting others where they are in their walks with the Lord. After all, when we all reach heaven, the only thing that will matter is glorifying God and His Son, Jesus.

–MK

Prayer

Lord, help me to be humble when my beliefs differ from others. I want to live my life in light of eternity so I won't waste time with what is not important. Help me to cultivate a gentle heart as I interact with those who are different from me. Amen.

For further study ~ Romans 15:1-13

Standing Before the Throne

Will family or friends gathering for showers or the birth of my baby cause a possibility for spiritual differences to arise? How can I prepare ahead of time to walk in gentleness and humility?

_____

_____

_____

_____

How can I glorify God by encouraging others even though we have differences?

_____

_____

_____

_____

What character qualities should I display that would encourage unity within the Body of Christ?

_____

_____

_____

_____

How good and pleasant it is when
brothers live together in unity!
~ Psalm 133:1

Anger

*For man's anger does not bring about
the righteous life that God desires.*
James 1:20

When I envision my life with my new child, I have television commercial dreams. You know, the ones that bring tears to your eyes: the mother gently rocking her sleeping baby. The baby lying in his mother's arms and reaching up to touch her face. The mother lifting her baby up high as they both giggle. Yes, that's what comes to mind when I think of my baby.

Much of our time will be spent in moments like these. But our lives will also include other scenes—scenes that don't have the sounds of gentle lullabies in the background. Scenes we won't want to capture forever.

Our children will test our patience. Our children will frustrate our plans. There will be times when we are angry at them.

Wait one minute! Do we need to think about these things now? Our babies haven't even been born yet! Certainly it is a little early to dwell on such serious issues.

But it's precisely because they are serious issues that it's never too early to think about them. Being a mother is one of the most important jobs in the world, and how we fulfill our roles will have lasting effects not only on ourselves, but also on our children. It is best to be prepared and know our biblical job description before we begin, so that we are not led by our emotions in a time of crisis. It is easier to continue good habits than break bad ones.

In the Bible, God shows us how to treat others. Because our children are precious people, made in the image of God, these standards also apply to our relationships with them. The Bible is therefore an excellent manual for mothers.

When our children willfully disobey us, when they seemingly do everything in their power to make our day miserable, it is tempting to give full vent to our anger. And on the surface, that may seem to work. If we yell at our children, or ridicule them, they may obey us. That makes this option even more tempting—it gets the job done. But does our anger truly accomplish godly goals, or does it put a temporary patch on a festering problem?

When we express anger toward our children, no matter what form it takes—yelling, name calling, throwing things, the silent treatment—there are certain consequences. First, we have disobeyed the Scripture that tells us to "let [our] gentleness be evident to all" (Philippians 4:5). Second, we are teaching our children by our example that this behavior is acceptable. Third, we are leading our children into the same sin.

"A gentle answer turns away wrath, but a harsh word stirs up anger" (Proverbs 15:1). Do we want to stir up anger in our children? It's a biblical promise that our harsh words will. "But if anyone causes one of these little ones who believe in me to sin, it would be better for him to have a large millstone hung around his neck and to be drowned in the depths of the sea" (Matthew 18:6).

What do we do if our children are the ones throwing out the harsh words and yelling at us? How should we respond? The answer is the same: with gentleness. We need to remember that our children are naturally more immature than we are. They need someone that loves them enough to take the time to teach them how to handle their temptations in a biblical manner. We have our children for about eighteen years and we see them almost every day. Who on earth, besides us, will ever have as much love or as much time to help them?

—MLG

Prayer

Father, thank You for bringing these issues to my attention now. I want to be the best mother I can and part of that is preparing to lead my child biblically. Help me to not look to the world for my parenting guidelines, but may I rely on the truths found in Your Word. Amen.

For further study ~ Genesis 4:1-8

Anger in My Life

Do others consider me a gentle person? I will ask these three people and record their responses:

_____

_____

_____

What are the situations where I am most tempted to be led by my emotions instead of being led by the Spirit?

_____

_____

_____

What types of books or magazines have I been reading to prepare me to raise this child? Are these wise choices?

_____

_____

_____

_____

Do not be quickly provoked in your spirit,
for anger resides in the lap of fools.
~ Ecclesiastes 7:9

Our Call to Share the Gospel

I came to you in weakness and fear, and with much trembling.
My message and my preaching were not with wise and
persuasive words, but with a demonstration of the Spirit's power.
1 Corinthians 2:3-4

As Christians, we know we are to be sharing the gospel with others. But whom exactly should we be telling about Jesus? Should we go knocking door-to-door every Saturday afternoon, or only share with our friends? Should we try to turn casual conversations at the grocery store into opportunities to evangelize, or wait for people to ask us questions? Whatever differing opinions we may have on this issue, one thing is clear for all of us: we are called to share the gospel with our children.

Too often, this role gets delegated to pastors and teachers in the church. Is this what God intended? Ephesians 4:11-12 says, "It was he who gave some to be apostles, some to be prophets, some to be evangelists, and some to be pastors and teachers, to prepare God's people for works of service, so that the body of Christ may be built up." Their job isn't just to do the work. Their job is to prepare us to do it, too.

"These commandments that I give you today are to be upon your hearts. Impress them on your children. Talk about them when you sit at home and when you walk along the road, when you lie down and when you get up" (Deuteronomy 6:6-7). It is our responsibility and our privilege to tell our children about the Lord and His commandments.

It's interesting that this passage from Deuteronomy refers to "these commandments," which are the Ten Commandments given to Moses on Mt. Sinai. Won't it be too harsh on our children if we dwell on these commandments, you might ask. Won't our children be frustrated and feel like an unreachable standard has been set?

The good news is...The Good News. When we teach the Ten Commandments to our children they will see where they fall short—that there is no way they can live up to sinless perfection and earn their way to heaven. Then we can point them to Christ. One cannot appreciate the good news until he knows the bad news. To be saved you have to know what you're being saved from.

The gospel does not demand eloquent speech or theological degrees. The gospel is simply the truth that God's wrath upon sinners was wiped away by the sacrifice of Christ on the cross. He humbly took the penalty of our sins upon Himself so that we who confess Him as Lord may be free from the flames of hell and walk in the joy of living for Him.

Let's not shrink back from our role as parents. Let's teach our children the Bible and point them to Christ. May we embrace the following passage as part of our job description:

"My purpose is that they may be encouraged in heart and united in love, so that they may have the full riches of complete understanding, in order that they may know the mystery of God, namely, Christ, in whom are hidden all the treasures of wisdom and knowledge" (Colossians 2:2-3).

–MLG

Prayer

Father, I willingly embrace the responsibility and privilege of teaching my child about You. It seems an overwhelming task, but I trust You and ask the Spirit to empower me. Please begin preparing me even now, Lord. Amen.

For further study ~ Philippians 1:3-11

My Call to Share the Gospel

Who shared the gospel with me?

_____

_____

_____

Am I equipped to share the gospel? What can I be doing now to prepare?

_____

_____

_____

_____

Here is my prayer for my child that she will one day be saved and know the joy of serving God:

_____

_____

_____

_____

_____

How, then, can they call on the one they have not believed in? And how can they believe in the one of whom they have not heard? And how can they hear without someone preaching to them?
~ Romans 10:14

What Am I Saying?

Do not let any unwholesome talk come out of your mouths, but only what is helpful for building others up according to their needs, that it may benefit those who listen.
Ephesians 4:29

I was so excited! Not only was I going out on a date tonight with my husband, but I also had something new to wear. A knit dress in black, the "slimming color." I was just putting on my lipstick when my 8-year-old walked into the bathroom and stared at me in the mirror.

"Oh," she said. "I expected you to wear something nice since you're going out with Daddy, but I forgot when you're pregnant you have to wear those kinds of clothes." Then without another word, she turned and walked out of the room.

My daughter is only a child, but there are many Christian adults that feel compelled to comment on other people's clothes, houses, marriages, children, finances...whatever. To justify themselves, they often refer to Ephesians 4:25: "Therefore each of you must put off falsehood and speak truthfully to his neighbor, for we are all members of one body," or Ephesians 4:15 which says we are to speak "the truth in love."

Yes, we are to speak the truth to each other. But if we honestly evaluate our words, we find that in most cases what we are speaking is not the truth— it is our opinion. And there's a big difference between the two.

Consider the example of my daughter and me. She could easily claim that there was nothing wrong with what she said, that she was just making a truthful comment. But it was not true that what I was wearing wasn't nice. It was her opinion. Too often we dress our views in shrouds of truth, but underneath it is still just opinion.

What's wrong with sharing our opinions? After all, the world praises those who are outspoken and feel free to speak their minds.

But what does God say? "A fool...delights in airing his own opinions"

(Proverbs 18:2). Are we so wise in our own eyes that we have become fools? James 1:26 says, "If anyone considers himself religious and yet does not keep a tight rein on his tongue, he deceives himself and his religion is worthless." Let's make sure that our religion—our belief in Christ—changes our whole life, even our tongue.

–MLG

Prayer

Lord, give me wisdom when I speak. Help me to judge whether I am speaking the truth or just speaking my opinion. Amen.

For further study ~ Matthew 12:33–37

Have I Been Acting Like a Fool?

Whom do I know who uses her tongue wisely — "building up others and benefiting those who listen"?

_____

_____

_____

_____

_____

Am I known for speaking my opinion? Or am I known for speaking the truth of the Lord?

_____

_____

_____

_____

_____

In considering conversations I've had this week, have the words of my mouth built up others? Who can I encourage today?

_____

_____

_____

_____

Set a guard over my mouth, O Lord; keep
watch over the door of my lips.
~ Psalm 141:3

Burdens or Blessings?

Come to me, all you who are weary and burdened, and I will give you rest. Take my yoke upon you and learn from me, for I am gentle and humble in heart, and you will find rest for your souls. For my yoke is easy and my burden is light.
Matthew 11:28-30

"I am exhausted from toting around these extra twenty pounds," I mumbled as I walked into the nursery.

"I can't do this!" I exclaimed to no one in particular as I surveyed the contents of the room. To go somewhere I would need to carry the infant car seat, port-a-crib, stroller and diaper bag. Add that to a seven-pound baby and my load more than doubles. "I just don't think I can do it!"

God gives us many blessings in our Christian walk. Many are easy for us to accept because of the obvious benefits. Yet, every blessing we receive can come with some measure of burden, depending upon our perspective and devotion to maintaining that blessing. A large house with a huge, beautifully landscaped yard needs someone to regularly care for it. That fixer-upper dream home needs someone to do the fixing. Even increased responsibility in the church can become a burden if we struggle with time management and working well with others.

We will have times of feeling burdened by our new babies. Today we are worrying about carrying all the paraphernalia. Soon, it might be trying to function with a lack of sleep. Who knows what might bring us to the weary and burdened edge. When that happens, what will we do?

Whenever we hit that edge, Christ is right there to help us. Jesus does not condemn us for these feelings; instead He understands how difficult life as a new mom can be.

Jesus is gentle and humble in heart. He is eager to let us take His yoke and learn from Him. He doesn't want us to run and hide—He wants us to run to Him. In the arms of Jesus we will find rest for our souls. When we face life with His provisions, the burden is light and the yoke is easy.

–MK

Prayer

Lord Jesus, help me when I feel burdened by the blessings that You give me. I want to carry only Your burden which is light and Your yoke which is easy. Amen.

For further study ~ Galatians 5:1–13

Burdens or Blessings?

What "blessings" have I complained about lately?

_____

_____

_____

_____

What should I do when I feel burdened?

_____

_____

_____

_____

This is how I feel after walking through the instructions of Matthew 11:28-30 and exchanging my burdens for the light and easy yoke Jesus promised:

_____

_____

_____

_____

Therefore, there is now no condemnation for those who are in Christ Jesus, because through Christ Jesus the law of the Spirit of life set me free from the law of sin and death.
~ Romans 8:1-2

Gentle as a Butterfly

By the meekness and gentleness of Christ, I appeal to you.
2 Corinthians 10:1

She quietly flits and gently lands
Upon a rose petal, she lightly fans.
From within the rose she draws its nectar
The hand of God is a butterfly protector.

Within my womb God quietly forms
A tiny life He gently warms.
God loves and nourishes with special nectar
The hand of God is my baby's protector.

Outwardly the beauty glows
While inwardly my baby grows.
God's gentleness is my nectar
The hand of God is a mother's protector.

How beautiful is a butterfly as she quietly lights on a flower. You never hear a sound, yet that adds to her beauty. There is nothing harsh or annoying about a butterfly. Perhaps that's why the first time we feel our babies within us it is like the fluttering of butterflies. No one else can feel it. It is a moment of intimacy—the gentle touch of God.

As quietly as a butterfly goes about her tasks, God gently and carefully works within the womb. The gentle hand of God encloses a baby in a protective bubble perforated only by the umbilical cord, the link of life to the mother. A miracle is forming in the secret place. An outward beauty radiates from the depths of creativity.

We are surrounded by the gentle hand of God, strengthening us to sustain another life. He empowers us, in the Holy Spirit's grace, to cultivate gentle hearts in preparation for motherhood. The gentle and quiet spirit of motherhood enhances our true beauty.

"Your beauty should not come from outward adornment, such as braided hair and the wearing of gold jewelry and fine clothes. Instead, it should be that of your inner self, the unfading beauty of a gentle and quiet spirit, which is of great worth in God's sight" (1 Peter 3:3-4).

–MK

Prayer

Father, what a beautiful thing it is to be pregnant. Prepare me to be a gentle mother. Help me to become more beautiful as I meditate on Your meekness and gentleness. Amen.

For Further Study ~ Ephesians 3:14-21

My Gentle Butterflies

I first felt my baby fluttering in my womb when…

_____

_____

_____

_____

_____

Do I see myself as beautiful in God's eyes? Why or why not?

_____

_____

_____

_____

How is God preparing me to be a gentle and quiet woman?

_____

_____

_____

_____

_____

Let your gentleness be evident
to all. The Lord is near.
~ Philippians 4:5

Pregnancy Prayer

I prayed for this child, and the Lord has granted me what I asked of him.
1 Samuel 1:27

Have you ever had this happen: You're in the middle of telling a friend all of the exciting details of your pregnancy, when you suddenly notice her squirming. What could be wrong, you innocently wonder?

It may be that your friend is struggling to rejoice with you. There are many women who long to have a baby and find that hearing about someone else's pregnancy is a reminder of what they don't have.

I have been on both sides of these conversations. Now that I am pregnant it amazes me how easily I forget the pain of waiting. When I was the one without a baby all I wanted to do was ask, "Why not me, Lord?"

It is good to get caught up in the joy of pregnancy and all the changes taking place. But we need to remember that others might look at our joy differently; maybe through eyes of longing or even hopelessness. We need to be gentle with our words, being considerate of what others might be feeling.

Because of pregnancy, we may not be able to clean a sick person's house or help a friend move. One thing we can do, though, is pray for couples who long to have children. We can ask God to open their wombs and give them peace in the waiting process.

You may be extremely fertile and not particularly overjoyed to find yourself having another child. There are many women who would give anything to be in your maternity clothes. Once again, we can use our pregnancy to remind us to pray for someone longing for a child.

Taking our eyes off of our own difficulties and putting our focus on others not only builds up the body of Christ, but it gives us a sense of accomplishment. Our prayers can make a difference in the lives of others.

What a joy it could be to join with another woman in praying for a child and be able to see the fruit of our prayers.

–MK

Prayer

Lord, I pray for couples who long to experience the joy that You have given me. When I am tempted to complain, help me to pray for women who would love to be pregnant. Let me pray for them as if I were in their situations. Amen.

For further study ～1 Samuel 1:1-20

Praying for Others

Have I been insensitive to any of my friends in what I have shared about this pregnancy? If so, what can I do to make it right?

_____

_____

_____

_____

_____

These are the couples I know who want a baby and have not been able to conceive:

_____

_____

_____

_____

Here is my prayer for those listed above:

_____

_____

_____

_____

_____

Be joyful in hope, patient in affliction, faithful in prayer.
~ Romans 12:12

Dirt from the World

Having loved his own who were in the world,
he now showed them the full extent of his love...so he got up
from the meal, took off his outer clothing, and wrapped
a towel around his waist. After that, he poured water into
a basin and began to wash his disciples' feet, drying them with
the towel that was wrapped around him.
John 13:1, 4-5

"Hi. Come on in. Sure, you can see the baby. Whoa, wait a minute. You can't hold her yet. You need to wash your hands first."

"Here you go. She really likes this pacifier. Oh! Pick it up quickly. I'll go boil some water to sterilize it."

When we bring our babies home, it's amazing how hard we try to keep everything clean. It seemed like I spent the first three months washing my hands, sterilizing bottles, and washing my baby's clothes—in specially-formulated detergent for babies, of course. Why do we go to so much effort? Is it because we have tons of free time on our hands and are looking for things to do? Certainly not. We do it because our babies are priceless treasures and we want to protect them.

We have a priceless treasure in us now. One that is even more valuable than the babies in our wombs. It is the Spirit of God. "Don't you know that you yourselves are God's temple and that God's Spirit lives in you?" (1 Corinthians 3:16). Imagine that! Wherever we go, whatever we do, we are carrying the Spirit of God within us. Most of the time, this is a comfort to me. But there are times when I just don't feel clean enough for this calling.

As Christians, we do not belong to the world, but we are to live in it (John 15:19). And by walking in the world and interacting with those in the world, we will get dirty. If we are around people at work that curse all day, then those words will lodge in our brains. If we see an immoral scene on a billboard, then that image will remain in our minds. If we are riding on a bus and surrounded by people gossiping, then those words will stick in our thoughts. We don't want to bring these things home with us. We don't want these things clinging to the temple of God's Spirit. So what can we do?

Take a look at John, chapter 13. In this passage, Jesus is with His disciples. As was the custom of the day, people wore sandals as they walked along the dusty roads. Therefore, when they arrived at their destination, their feet were dirty from the world. Usually it was the job of the slaves to wash the travelers' feet.

On this particular day, though, Jesus got up from the table and wrapped a towel around his waist. It is with gentleness that we see Jesus bending in front of each of His disciples and tenderly washing their feet. The Son of God willingly became a servant to show them the depth of His love.

Jesus still washes feet today. When we have been in the world and exposed to its harsh elements, we can turn to our Lord to cleanse us. Not only can we turn to the Lord, we need to turn to the Lord to cleanse us. Because we have the Spirit of God within us, we can not let these things linger in our minds. They will darken our hearts and lessen our discernment. We need to daily bring our soiled minds before the Lord and ask Him to wash them clean.

John 13:14 records Jesus as saying, "Now that I, your Lord and Teacher, have washed your feet, you also should wash one another's feet." We are to follow Jesus' example by humbling ourselves and gently washing each other's feet. Some ways we can do this are praying and sharing the Word of God with each other. The key, though, is the gentleness in which these acts of love are expressed—gentleness that stems from humility. Jesus said, "I am gentle and humble in heart" (Matthew 11:29). May we be able to say the same.

–MLG

Prayer

Lord, I thank You for the ways You have demonstrated Your love to me. Thank You for the examples in the Bible that give me a clear picture of Your heart. Cleanse me, Lord, from the worldliness that I am exposed to and help me to follow in Your steps as I learn to gently wash the feet of others. Amen.

For further study ~ Philippians 2:5-11

Cleanse Me, Lord

What things am I regularly exposed to that cling to my heart and mind?

_____

_____

When considering where to go and what to do, are my decisions based on the fact that I am carrying the Spirit of God within me? In what ways have my actions reflected this knowledge, or lack thereof?

_____

_____

Whose feet has God called me to wash?

_____

_____

...and is well known for her good deeds, such as bringing up children, showing hospitality, washing the feet of the saints, helping those in trouble and devoting herself to all kinds of good deeds.
~1 Timothy 5:10

Patience

*And the one on whom seed was sown on the good soil,
this is the man who hears the word and understands it,
who indeed bears fruit, and brings forth, some a hundredfold,
some sixty, and some thirty.*

Matthew 13:23 NASB

What's Taking So Long?

The Lord is not slow in keeping his promise, as some understand slowness. He is patient with you, not wanting anyone to perish, but everyone to come to repentance.
2 Peter 3:9

"When are you due?"

"Last week," I reply with a smirk.

With each pregnancy, I convince myself that I'm not going to get impatient toward the end. After all, the baby will eventually be born, and I should just enjoy the time she is safe (and quiet) in my belly. But each time, I begin counting the days till my due date, and then, with each of my pregnancies, I have also had to count the days after my due date — all the way up to ten days late.

"Late"? That's an odd term to use. Who says I'm "late"? The due date given by my doctor is just an educated guess based on the average pregnancy. But my pregnancy, and my baby, are not in the hands of my doctor. They are in the hands of the almighty God who created my baby. God does not follow my calendar or my doctor's calendar.

There are other times when I'm tempted to think the Lord is late: when I see the evil in this world, when I read about the endless murders of the unborn, when I see the wicked seem to go unpunished and when I see God mocked in the media. I want to cry out, "Lord, where are You? Surely, this is the end of the world that You described. Aren't You coming back? Why are You waiting?"

2 Peter 3:9 makes it clear, though, that what I am seeing is the Lord's patience. Because on the day that He returns, those who have given their lives to Christ will be taken up, and those who have trusted in anything else will be left behind. "Whoever tries to keep his life will lose it, and whoever loses his life will preserve it. I tell you, on that night two people will be in one bed; one will be taken and the other left" (Luke 17:33-34).

The day the Lord returns will be a time of terror for many people. But as

Christians, we can be thankful for our own salvation. We can see the events of the world, spinning seemingly out of control, yet know that the Lord is patient because He wishes all to come to repentance. We can join with Christians all over the world and pray for others and for the leaders of our countries.

Even though we do not understand everything, we know that the Lord's timing is perfect, from our pregnancies to the second coming of Christ. We can rest in the fact that He has everything in His hands.

–MLG

Prayer

Lord, I would truly be lost without You. I am not only thankful that I will one day join You in heaven, I am also thankful that Your Spirit is with me every day on earth, guiding my life and guiding my pregnancy. Thank You for Your patience with me and the world. Amen.

For further study ~ Matthew 24:36-51

The Lord Is Patient

In what areas of my life do I try to rush the Lord, thinking that my timing is better than His?

_____

_____

_____

_____

In what ways has this pregnancy showed me that the Lord is in control?

_____

_____

_____

_____

When I see the unsaved doing evil in this world, am I thankful that the Lord is patient because He does not want anyone to perish? Or do I wish they would be quickly judged and get what they "deserve"? Am I patient and merciful like the Lord?

_____

_____

_____

_____

Because judgment without mercy will be shown to anyone who has not been merciful. Mercy triumphs over judgment!
~ James 2:13

Honor Your Father and Your Mother

Honor your father and your mother, so that you may live long in the land the Lord your God is giving you.
Exodus 20:12

"Don't tell me what to do!"

That was my anthem as a teenager. Regretfully, things haven't changed much. The cry of my heart is now: "Don't tell me how to raise my children!"

I thought that because I was pregnant and about to become a mother, it would be easy for my parents to see me as an adult and able to make wise decisions concerning my child. I assumed that their plans for this child would just fall in line behind mine. I was wrong.

What are we to do when we go from being someone's child to being someone's mother? Do we forsake our first role to fulfill our second? How should we interact with our parents now that we are parents, too? More importantly, how should we interact considering that we are Christians?

We can start with the command that says to honor our father and our mother. There are no age limitations on this command. As long as we have a father and a mother, we are to honor them.

Becoming parents ourselves may make it easier to honor our parents. We can begin to understand their perspectives a little more. Plus, the baby opens up more opportunities to bless our parents. We can keep them posted on our monthly visits to the obstetrician and show them sonogram pictures. We can ask our parents to tell us stories about when we were young and show us photos.

Once the baby is born, we can keep our parents involved by giving them pictures, sending them cards from the baby on special occasions, and including them when possible on family outings.

What should we do when our parents give us advice about the baby? If it is helpful, we should thank them and apply the advice. But what about advice that does not line up with Scripture? How do we balance the command to honor our parents with the responsibility to raise our children according to the Word of God?

The answer is found in the book of Matthew. Jesus says the greatest commandment is to "Love the Lord your God with all your heart and with all your soul and with all your mind" (Matthew 22:37). Our allegiance is first and foremost to the Lord. We need to raise our children in such a way that reflects our devotion and obedience to Him. We are still called to honor our parents, but we no longer have a responsibility to obey them.

As we read further, though, Jesus follows this commandment with what He calls the second greatest commandment: "Love your neighbor as yourself" (Matthew 22:39). Our parents are also our neighbors in the eyes of the Lord. This makes the standard easy to comprehend. We are to treat our parents like we want to be treated by our own children.

So if our parents give us advice that we see as unbiblical, we listen patiently and gently explain to them our position. "Therefore, as God's chosen people, holy and dearly loved, clothe yourselves with compassion, kindness, humility, gentleness and patience" (Colossians 3:12). Our parents are also going through an adjustment period as grandparents. We need to be patient with them as they get used to their new roles in our lives.

That doesn't mean our parents will instantly see the wisdom in our decisions, and it doesn't mean the issues will not come up again. What it does mean, though, is that we can have a clear conscience before the Lord that we handled the situation in a manner that is pleasing to Him.

–MLG

Prayer

Lord, I want to be a godly mother and a godly daughter. Please help me to balance these two roles. I want to raise my child according to the convictions You have given me; yet I also want to honor my parents and their role as grandparents. Amen.

For further study ~ Luke 2:41-50

Honoring My Father and My Mother

The first place to start is with thankfulness. I'm glad I even have a father and/or a mother, and I appreciate these specific qualities about them:

_____

_____

_____

Have I exhibited patience with my parents? How can I prepare myself to be patient in the future?

_____

_____

_____

If my father and mother are no longer living, whom do I know who would enjoy being my child's "adopted grandparents"?

_____

_____

If it is possible, as far as it depends
on you, live at peace with everyone.
~ Romans 12:18

The Last Delivery

Be still before the Lord and wait patiently for him.
Psalm 37:7

Three of my friends were pregnant. Our due dates lined up in a row: the 24th, 26th, 28th and 30th. The first one went into labor on the 24th. Then it was my turn…or so I thought, until I was sent home with Braxton-Hicks contractions. When the other two friends went into labor, it got more and more difficult to face the comments: "I thought you went into labor. When are you due?" "Isn't it about time you had that baby?"

I longed to hold my newborn in my arms. Believe me, if there was something I could have done to make it happen, I would have done it. Yet all I could do was wait.

There is nothing more frustrating for a person who loves to be in control than a situation that puts her totally out of control. When the first of the month came, I thought God was going to leave me pregnant for the rest of my life. If I gained any more weight I would burst. Yet God always knew the precise moment when He would bring forth this child.

When the day finally arrived, it was my easiest delivery. Quick, even though she was nearly ten pounds! God had a plan from the start.

As we wait on God to bring forth our children, the process develops the fruit of patience. Being a mother will require patience, and pregnancy is preparation for motherhood. He will teach us to wait, and to trust in His timing.

–MK

Prayer

You are a patient God. You love me even when I impatiently wait on Your timing. Help me to rest in You, to be still and content waiting for Your blessing. Open my eyes to see the blessings You unfold for me while I wait. Amen.

For Further Study ~ Romans 8:18-25

Waiting for Delivery

How have I lacked patience during this pregnancy?

_____

_____

_____

_____

_____

_____

_____

How does Scripture compare to what is in my heart as I wait?

_____

_____

_____

_____

_____

_____

_____

What blessings has God revealed as I wait patiently for His timing?

_____

_____

_____

_____

_____

_____

_____

_____

I am still confident of this:
I will see the goodness of the Lord in
the land of the living. Wait for the Lord; be
strong and take heart and wait for the Lord.
~ Psalm 27:13-14

How Long, Lord?

*The end of a matter is better than its
beginning, and patience is better than pride.*
Ecclesiastes 7:8

The grocery store grew quiet as I stepped out of line and waddled over to the scale. Most people have a natural curiosity to try and get a glimpse of someone's weight. I suppose when it comes to seeing how much a pregnant lady weighs, the lure is irresistible. I stepped on the scale, quickly glanced at the numbers, gulped, trudged back, and loudly proclaimed to my husband, "Wow, that's amazing. The baby weighs forty pounds!"

Okay, I know my baby didn't weigh that much. I realize that he will probably only weigh about eight pounds when he is born. But I am convinced that while he is still within me, he is close to forty pounds. What else could possibly explain the numbers on the scale?

Actually, the explanation is perfectly clear. Not only is there a baby growing inside of me, but my own body has also been getting larger. And that is what's challenging for me. If I only gained an amount proportionate to the size of my baby, it wouldn't be so hard. But I gain a lot, and I gain it everywhere. My belly is just one of the areas expanding. My face, legs, breasts, arms, feet and hips are also growing. And when this baby is born, I know these areas won't just naturally shrink back down. I love babies, but I do not love watching my body swell for nine long months. If it was only quicker!

And that is where the verse above speaks to me: "…And patience is better than pride." All of my grumbling and complaining is about one thing: my looks. Instead of letting my pride rule my attitude, I should be patient during this season. I know that God created my body to work this way, and I know that the gift He has in store for me is well worth whatever price I have to pay.

Patience is not the same as passivity, though. We should not plop down on the couch and wait patiently for God to deliver our babies. Instead, we need to be preparing our bodies for what lies ahead.

This begins with making sure that we are eating healthy foods. We are the only source of nutrition for our babies, and we need to be careful about the choices we make. There are some things we should not eat during pregnancy. This is another chance to exhibit patience during this season.

Besides our eating habits, we need to evaluate our exercise program. Ladies, we are about to be in a marathon. Who knows the number of hours it will take to deliver these babies? And the race doesn't stop there! We will then need to keep up a rigorous schedule of physical exertion and broken sleep as we care for our newborns. We will need cardiovascular strength and physical endurance — two things which only come through training. That's not accomplished by pushing ourselves like an athlete, but faithfully doing those exercises approved by our doctors. The results may not be evident when we look at our bodies, but we need to continue on with patience, knowing that we will reap the benefits later.

We want to work with the bodies that God has given us, not resent them. There is no perfect weight gain, no perfect eating plan, no perfect exercise program, no perfect mom. With the Lord's help, though, we need to do the best we can to care for our bodies so that we can then care for our babies.

–MLG

Prayer

Father, help me to be patient through this season. You know exactly how long my baby needs to grow inside my womb and You make no mistakes. Please help me to get my body in the best condition to provide for my child, both while he is inside me, and once he is born. Amen.

For further study ~ James 5:7-11

How Long, Lord?

In what areas during this pregnancy have I been tempted to be impatient?

_____

_____

_____

_____

What does my attitude reveal about how I view my body during pregnancy?

_____

_____

_____

_____

In what ways have I been preparing my body for labor and caring for a newborn? In what ways do I need to change?

_____

_____

_____

_____

Being strengthened with all power according to his glorious might so that you may have great endurance and patience, and joyfully giving thanks to the Father, who has qualified you to share in the inheritance of the saints in the kingdom of light.
~ Colossians 1:11-12

A Friend Loves at All Times

Perfume and incense bring joy to the heart, and the pleasantness of one's friend springs from his earnest counsel.
Proverbs 27:9

My hormones were raging and I was angry at the world. I ignored the ringing phone until I heard the voice on the answering machine. It was a dear friend from junior high school. We were friends before we were Christians and our friendship grew deeper after Jesus became Lord of our lives. How did she know that I needed a friend now more than I needed to let my hormones rage?

I picked up the phone and shared my heart with her. From over a thousand miles away, she encouraged me and prayed for me. She reminded me of the time I visited her when she was nine months pregnant with her seventh child, and her hormones were raging. I counseled her then. She was counseling me now.

Friendships — we need them. Women understand women. Especially one who has been, or is, pregnant. As you read this, most likely a friend or two has popped into your mind. One who has been there for you. One who has loved you through difficult circumstances. One whom you call when you need encouragement.

Maybe you have just moved. All of your friends are far away and you have not had a chance to build new relationships. No matter where we are or what our circumstances, we always have a Friend just a whisper away: Jesus. He understands us better than anyone. He says, "You are my friends if you do what I command. I no longer call you servants, because a servant does not know his master's business. Instead, I have called you friends, for everything that I learned from my Father I have made known to you" (John 15:14-15). Jesus shares His Father's heart with us, and we can share our hearts with Him.

If we ask Him, He can send us a dear friend. He is willing to give us whatever we wish (John 15:7). So if a friend is the desire of your heart, ask God for someone with whom you can share your life. If you have a close friend, give her a call and set a time to get together.

Next time hormones are raging, or doubts are forming, or you just long for a close friend, go to God in prayer. Seek His direction. Then ask Him with whom you can share your heart. Another sister in the Lord may be praying for your fellowship. God gave us these desires for friendship. Don't miss out on the joy of calling a friend!

–MK

Prayer

Jesus, You are my Friend. You are there when no one else is. Thank You, God, for the gift of friendship. I pray for friends to share my heart with, to help me through hard times, and to share great moments with. You know what I need and when I need it. You know whom I need to have relationships with. Thank You that You consider me Your friend. Help me to be a friend. Amen.

For further study ~ 1 Samuel 20

My Friendships

Jesus is my Friend. This is the heart issue I need to take to Him right now:

_____

_____

What friend came to mind while reading this? When was the last meaningful time I had with her?

_____

_____

Here is a story of a time when I was able to help a friend or a friend helped me in a time of need:

_____

_____

_____

_____

_____

_____

_____

_____

And the scripture was fulfilled that says,
"Abraham believed God, and it was
credited to him as righteousness," and he
was called God's friend.
~ James 2:23

Authority

Wives, submit to your husbands as to the Lord. For the husband is the head of the wife as Christ is the head of the church, his body, of which he is the Savior. Now as the church submits to Christ, so also wives should submit to their husbands in everything.
Ephesians 5:22-24

*M*y husband placed his hand on my womb and began praying for me. Suddenly he stopped. "I just felt the baby move!" he cried out. I hadn't felt it yet, but when I laid my hand on my stomach, I felt the movement as well.

"That's not fair!" I grumbled. "I should have been the first to feel my baby move." But that was really selfishness on my part. I get nine months of almost exclusive rights to my baby, while my husband has to hear about it second-hand. What a special gift from God for my husband to feel the baby's first movement!

My baby's first known response was to his daddy. It was a powerful reminder that although my husband has not been given the privilege to carry this child within him, he is the authority over this child and our home.

Does my husband retain his authority at all times? What about when we enter the delivery room? Who will be the authority then? The answer is still the same. Not the doctor, not the nurse, not the midwife. It is my husband, under the authority of Christ.

We hire professionals with the knowledge and training to help us maintain our health and the health of our babies. But our husbands are the ones with the God-given authority to make the final decisions. Even if our spouses are not Christians, God can speak through them. If the baby's father is not a part of our lives, then we are to go straight to God. He is our spouse when our spiritual covering is not there (Isaiah 54:5).

Resting in the headship of our husbands will bring peace to labor and delivery. Discussing beforehand as many choices as we can will reassure us that our husbands know what we want or don't want. We need to make sure we discuss options, desires and decisions with our doctors or midwives before the heat of the moment.

While we pray that no complications arise, we need to prepare for the unexpected. Jesus is able to speak in the midst of the storm and may even speak differently than we prepared. We can trust God to work through our imperfect spouses. Then we will be free to focus on delivering our babies.

–MK

Prayer

Lord, I trust You to lead my husband as he leads me. Life and death decisions may have to be made during delivery. Please give my husband discernment to hear Your counsel and the courage to boldly speak what is best for our family. Amen.

For further study ~ 1 Peter 3:1-6

My Husband's Authority

These are the desires and options my husband and I have decided we want for labor and delivery:

_____

_____

_____

_____

Do I struggle with submitting to my husband's authority? In what ways do I see evidence of this?

_____

_____

_____

I don't have a husband. I have chosen _____ to help me make important decisions concerning my baby's birth. I chose this person because...

_____

_____

_____

*Then they can train the younger women
to love their husbands and children, to be
self-controlled and pure, to be busy at home,
to be kind, and to be subject to their husbands,
so that no one will malign the word of God.
~ Titus 2:4–5*

Are We Ready?

*You also must be ready, because the Son of Man
will come at an hour when you do not expect him.
Luke 12:40*

I sat slouched on the couch like a beached whale. My rounded belly rested on what was left of my lap. My overnight bag was packed and by the front door, ready to be grabbed when the time came. The nursery was neatly arranged with all of the shower gifts in place. The final flurry of the nesting instinct had come and gone. I was ready.

I was prepared for the day when my child would come, but there is an even more important day to prepare for. A day that is unknown to everyone except God. The day Christ returns.

Are our spiritual bags packed, full of the wisdom of God? Do we have a clear conscience before God? Have we been faithful in the work that He has called us to do? Our actions do not earn our salvation, but if we have salvation, we will want to do the work of Christ up to our very last minute on earth.

Jesus commands us to be ready for His return (Matthew 24:44). In the book of Matthew, we read the parable of ten virgins (Matthew 25:1-13). They each had a lamp while waiting to meet the bridegroom, which symbolized Christ. The foolish ones took their lamps, but no extra oil. The wise took oil in jars along with their lamps. The wise virgins were ready for the long haul, prepared until the end. We do not want to be like the foolish virgins whose oil ran out in the final hour because the Master was long in coming. We want to be like the wise virgins whose oil will last. We want to be ready.

We know the approximate day that our babies will come. However, we don't know the day Jesus will come again (1 Thessalonians 4:16). God's Word says the coming of the Lord will happen as suddenly as labor pains on a pregnant woman (1 Thessalonians 5:3). Are we as prepared for Christ as we are for these babies? Are our hearts prepared even in this season (2 Timothy 4:2)?

These questions can only be answered by spending time with God in prayer and asking Him to show us our hearts. We don't want to be more concerned with the empty things of this world than with the eternal things of God. We do not want to be caught unaware on that final day.

If our hearts are willing to serve God and not ourselves, then we will be diligent in His work. If our hearts have strayed because of the cares of this world, we can take a minute right now and ask God to show us, not only where our hearts are, but also how to be prepared until the end.

–MK

Prayer

Father, only You know the day and the hour of the second coming. Help me to be prepared when Jesus comes again. I want to be a "wise virgin" by filling my "oil lamp" with Your wisdom and Your will every day so I will be ready on that final day. Amen.

For further study ~ Matthew 25:1-13

Am I Ready?

What things do I need to be doing now to prepare for my baby?

_____

_____

_____

_____

Would I consider myself like a wise virgin or a foolish virgin? How can I make sure my lamp is lit and my oil jar full?

_____

_____

Here are some areas where my heart has strayed from God and what I can do to bring my heart back to where it belongs:

_____

_____

_____

_____

He said to them: "It is not for
you to know the times or dates the Father
has set by his own authority."
~ Acts 1:7

Sanctification Motivation

Sanctify them by the truth; your word is truth. As you sent me into the world, I have sent them into the world. For them I sanctify myself, that they too may be truly sanctified.
John 17:17-19

I expected this pregnancy to change me. I knew my belly would grow, I knew my breasts would get larger, perhaps I expected my hips to widen a bit. But what I wasn't prepared for was how my heart would change.

Sure, I knew I would be grateful for this baby. I knew my eyes would brim with tears at the sight of a newborn in her mother's arms. I knew that holding someone else's baby would cause me to long for the day when I would cradle my own. But that's not even what I'm talking about. What I am referring to is my "open heart surgery" under the skillful hand of God Almighty Himself.

From the beginning of my pregnancy God has exposed my heart in the areas of fear, self-control, peace, patience, and the list goes on. He has faithfully used my raging hormones, nausea, fatigue and various aches and pains to reveal the condition of my heart. Did He show me all this to then just leave me on the operating table? No! He patiently led me through the truth of His Word so that I could change.

Just think what He will do with this relationship once the baby is born. God willing, I will have a lifetime of sanctification ahead of me.

One of the most effective tools to make us more like Christ is our children. Why? Because they are there. They are there when we wake up, they are there when we don't want to wake up. They are there when we are at our best and when we are at our worst.

Our children will see, when no one else is looking. They are built in accountability factors — our character will be reflected in them. If they see us standing firm and holding to God's teachings when things are difficult, then they are more likely to follow our example and stand firm. Our children will see us fail many times, for we are far from perfect. What we want them to learn from our mistakes is the godly way we repent and walk in forgiveness.

The process of sanctification is one of hope. It is a process in which we take the truths of the Word and faithfully work them out in our lives day after day. It is a process that we do not have to work out on our own. We need only to follow the example of Christ.

—MK

Prayer

Father, thank You for Your example as I train my heart, so that I may train my children. Help me to be an example of truth in this world. As You sanctify me, remind me often that my little motivators are watching me follow Your example. Fill me with Your grace when I fall short and encourage me with the hope of seeing myself and my children sanctified daily.

For further study ~ 2 Corinthians 3:12-18

My Sanctification Motivation

How has my baby brought sanctification into my life so far?

_____

_____

_____

_____

This is the truth that helped me in the process:

_____

_____

_____

_____

What area of my walk is in the process of sanctification now? How will this make me a better parent?

_____

_____

_____

_____

Now may the God of peace Himself sanctify you entirely; and may your spirit and soul and body be preserved complete, without blame at the coming of our Lord Jesus Christ. Faithful is He who calls you, and He also will bring it to pass. ~1 Thessalonians 5:23-24

Joy

God blessed them and said to them, "Be fruitful
and increase in number; fill the earth and subdue it."
Genesis 1:28

Praise to the Lord

From the lips of children and infants you have ordained praise because of your enemies, to silence the foe and the avenger.
Psalm 8:2

The sight was astounding. There, on the sonogram screen, I could see my adorable baby. After only four months in my womb, my baby already had arms and legs, fingers and toes. He lay on his back, feet up in the air, waving his arms around. What a joy to get a glimpse of this beautiful and active child in my womb.

Look at a picture of a baby in the womb and notice all of the intricate details. How can anyone see this and not believe in God? Watch a child's face light up as he calls out, "Mommy," and runs with arms open wide to hug her. Could a mother truly think her child was the result of some cosmic accident?

Children are one of the greatest testimonies to the existence of God. We know from Scripture that they praise God, as anyone who has heard a child pray can testify. But the power of their lives goes even farther. Children and infants not only praise God, but they inspire others to praise Him.

It's not only that we marvel at the intricate workings of a little baby's body, but the Lord often uses children to soften our hearts. When we gaze into the face of an infant, it's amazing how the things of the world seem to fade for a moment and we are filled with an unexplainable peace. When we see a child grin with delight, it's incredible how quickly that smile spreads to our face.

Truly, our Lord is a wondrous Creator, and children are an incredible gift from His hands.

–MLG

Prayer

Lord, I ask that You would use my baby to bring hope to a hopeless world. I pray that each person that holds my child will be reminded of Your love and power. And please, Lord, may I always be in awe of You when I gaze upon the miracle You have given me. Amen.

For further study ~ Psalm 139:1-18

May My Child
Bring Praise to Your Name

Whom do I know who needs the joy of holding a baby?

_____

_____

_____

_____

How can I be preparing now to share my baby with others?

_____

_____

_____

_____

How can the Lord use me to declare His glory at the obstetrician's office, hospital, birthing center, or pediatrician's office?

_____

_____

_____

_____

_____

*Before I formed you
in the womb I knew you.
~ Jeremiah 1:5*

A Vessel for the Lord

Behold, children are a gift of the Lord;
the fruit of the womb is a reward.
Psalm 127:3 NASB

I pushed away from my desk and hoisted myself up from the chair. I needed to stretch. Putting a phone book under my feet as I sat at the computer just wasn't helping today. As I waddled down the hallway to the break room, I felt like a fat blowfish swimming upstream against a school of sleek minnows. Ladies in sharp, tailored suits parted to the left and right to clear a path for me and the peach-colored muu-muu I was wearing. I heard the crisp click-click of their high heels as they energetically sped along. I looked down at my own shoes…oh, that's right…I can't see them. I was confident, though, that I had stuck my support-hosed feet into something called "sensible shoes." I am so tired of wearing tents! I am so tired of being swollen! I am so tired of being tired!

As I continued my trek down the hall, God interrupted my thoughts and reminded me of something I had lost sight of: I am carrying a child of God. Sure that may seem obvious, but it's easy to forget in the midst of sleepless nights, backaches, and stretch marks. God has placed a child in my womb. What an amazing thought! My husband and I had something to do with it, but we all know many couples "doing their part" yet still without a child. Psalm 139:13 says, "…you [God] knit me together in my mother's womb." It is not the "act" that places a child in the womb, it is the hand of the almighty God.

For some reason, God had chosen to place a child in my womb. And He has chosen to place a child in your womb. Did he do this to punish us? Was His desire to make us exhausted, fat, and irritable? No, His desire was to bless us. We are not only a temple for God's Spirit (1 Corinthians 3:16), we are also now a temple for a child of God. Our feet and hands are swelling because we are supporting little lives. Our chests are growing because they are preparing to nourish our babies. Our bellies are expanding because they are vessels for new human beings. Yes! These changes are good. Our bodies are working the way they are supposed to work. Thank You, Lord!

I straightened up my shoulders and lifted up my head a little as I stepped into the break room. I have a wonderful calling for my life and I do not want to grumble and complain. I'm on a mission from God, and I am thrilled to be carrying such precious cargo.

–MLG

Prayer

Father, thank You for placing a child in my womb. You didn't have to give me a baby; You just chose to bless me. Please forgive me for grumbling and complaining. May I delight in this call on my life, and remember that all the changes in my body are working toward a much greater good—supporting the life of my baby. What a small price to pay for such a tremendous gift! Amen.

For further study ~ Psalm 100

I Am an Uncommon Vessel

Am I allowing the sacrifices of pregnancy to overshadow the joy of bearing a child? Here is a list of my current complaints. Are any of them more important than having a child?

_____

_____

_____

When I look in the mirror, what do I see? A large, tired woman, or an incredible body created by God for a special purpose?

_____

_____

_____

Who am I allowing to shape my opinions? I want to renew my mind by meditating on Scripture. What would be a godly response to each of the complaints I listed in the first question?

_____

_____

_____

Therefore, I urge you, brothers, in view of God's mercy, to offer your bodies as living sacrifices, holy and pleasing to God — this is your spiritual act of worship.
~ Romans 12:1

What the World Needs Now

See to it that no one takes you captive through hollow and deceptive philosophy, which depends on human tradition and the basic principles of this world rather than on Christ.
Colossians 2:8

"With overcrowding, food shortages, and rampant evil, how can you bring another child into this world?"

My answer: "How could I not?"

For you see, I don't plan to bring another child into this world to drain the economy, destroy the environment, or terrorize the people. With God's grace, I plan to bring into this world a child who will know the words of God found in the Bible—a child who knows who created him and knows the call upon his life. I plan to bring into this world a child who learns to love the Lord his God with all his heart, soul, and mind, and learns to love his neighbor as himself (Matthew 22:37-38). This is the child I plan to bring into the world, and this is the child this world needs.

Think about it. When we as Christians have a child and bring him into a Christian home, God rejoices. But who is not pleased when a Christian gives birth? Don't you think the enemies of God want to thin our ranks and weaken our forces? One of the ways to accomplish this is to stop us from reproducing. Do not be deceived! God says in Genesis 1:22 that we are to be "fruitful and increase in number." Of course! We are the army of God. Whether we contribute one child or ten to His army, we are building His kingdom. The world, with what it falsely calls knowledge, may disagree with us, but 2 Corinthians 5:9 gives us the goal for our lives: "to please him."

So, let's not shrink back if someone questions the wisdom of our pregnancy. Let's keep the vision before us that what we are doing is more than increasing our family size. We are adding to something far greater than ourselves. We are building the army of God.

—MLG

Prayer

Lord, thank You that You have given me this child to raise for You. What an awesome privilege! Even while this child is still in my womb, help me to understand my role in Your eternal plans. Amen.

For further study ~1 Corinthians 1:18-31

The World Needs My Child

In what ways have I allowed the empty philosophies of the world to cloud my understanding of pregnancy?

_____

_____

_____

What negative feedback have I received concerning my pregnancy? How can I respond the next time?

_____

_____

_____

Here is a letter to my child that expresses my gratitude for being his mother and my excitement in looking forward to what God has planned for his life.

_____

_____

_____

_____

_____

Guard what has been entrusted to your care.
Turn away from godless chatter and the opposing
ideas of what is falsely called knowledge.
~1 Timothy 6:20

A Bundle of Joy

Discipline your son, and he will give you peace;
he will bring delight to your soul.
Proverbs 29:17

Congratulations! You're having a baby. It won't be long now until you will be able to hold your bundle of joy. He will have a smile that melts your heart. He will have an adorable little face that you love to kiss. He will have a laugh that brightens your day. He will have a scream that drives you crazy. He will have a mind of his own that rises up against you. He will have a temper that he chooses to display in public places.

Yes, your precious child will have one thing in common with all other children throughout the ages: he will sin (Romans 3:23). It's hard to believe, and it's not what we want to think about now, but it is true and we need to be prepared. I do not want to be formulating my parenting plan while I'm standing in a grocery store watching my toddler hurl cans of string beans down the aisle. I want a plan before the action begins.

There is no better place to turn than the Bible. It is a wealth of parenting wisdom. In it, we are told to "Train up a child in the way he should go, and when he is old he will not turn from it" (Proverbs 22:6). The word "train" is a verb and requires action on our part; parenting is not a spectator sport. Proverbs 29:15 says, "The rod of correction imparts wisdom, but a child left to himself disgraces his mother." Our children need us to teach them, discipline them, and show them by example what is right.

Will it be fun to discipline our children? Not at all. We do it, though, because we love them. We do it because they belong to God, and He has given us the responsibility of representing Him to our children. Ephesians 6:1 says, "Children, obey your parents in the Lord, for this is right." It is by obeying us that our children eventually learn to obey God.

We all want our children to be happy. The greatest way to ensure this is to teach them to love God with all their hearts and obey His commands. "But let all who take refuge in you be glad; let them ever sing for joy. Spread your protection over them, that those who love your name may rejoice in you. For surely, O Lord, you bless the righteous; you surround them with your favor as with a shield" (Psalm 5:11-12).

–*MLG*

Prayer

God, I thank You for this gift of joy You are giving me. I want to be faithful in raising my child, and disciplining him according to Your Word, so that he may know the true joy of a life with You. Amen.

For further study ~ Hebrews 12:5-11

Your Bundle of Joy

What do Proverbs 19:18 and Proverbs 22:15 say to me?

_____

_____

_____

_____

Even before my baby is born, I can begin preparing by getting in the habit of turning to the Bible for guidance in my own life. These issues have come up in my life this past week, and I found that Scripture says:

_____

_____

_____

Here is my vision for this child. I want to raise my child to:

_____

_____

To train him in this way, I will:

_____

_____

He who spares the rod hates his son,
but he who loves him is careful to discipline him.
~ Proverbs 13:24

Not Ashamed

*I am not ashamed of the gospel, because it is
the power of God for the salvation of everyone who
believes: first for the Jew, then for the Gentile.*
Romans 1:16

Do I plan to keep my baby's birth a secret? Will I keep her things out of sight? Will I try to hide the fact that having a baby has changed my whole life?

Of course not. I'll be like most mothers in the world: excited about my baby and taking advantage of every opportunity to talk about her. In fact, all my friends will know that my life has changed and I am now a mother.

Is this true about our relationship with Christ? Do all our friends know that we are Christians? Sure, they may know that we do kind things for others and don't cheat on our taxes, but do they know why? Do they know that we live for Christ and all the good things we do are ultimately because we love Him and want to obey Him? Or are we more comfortable leaving our friends with the impression that we are just nice people?

What about strangers? I can be at a store, or walking down a busy street, talking the whole time with a friend. But the minute the conversation turns to church or God, we immediately lower our voices. Why? Probably because we worry about what others will think. Would it really be that bad for some stranger standing next to us at the cash register to know that we are Christians? Maybe overhearing our conversation about God would encourage her in some way, or even prompt her to ask us where we go to church. The possibility for good clearly outweighs the risk of being ridiculed.

And besides that, don't we love God? Aren't we thankful that He saved us from our sins and turned our lives around? We believe in God. We believe Jesus is the Son of God, died for our sins, and was resurrected. We know the power and truth of His Word. This should not be discussed with hushed voices as if we were ashamed. This is something to be excited about. This is the gospel. This is good news!   —MLG

Prayer

Lord, please forgive me for the times when my actions show that I am ashamed of the gospel. In my heart, I am thankful for all You've done for me and want others to know about You. It is the cry of my heart, Lord, that I will be more concerned about what You think than what others think. Amen.

For further study ~ Mark 8:34-38

I Will Not Be Ashamed

When am I most likely to try and hide my faith?

_____

_____

_____

_____

Why?

_____

_____

_____

_____

I want to talk about the Lord just as excitedly as I talk about this baby.
Where can I begin today to talk more openly about my faith?

_____

_____

_____

_____

For God did not give us a spirit of timidity,
but a spirit of power, of love and of self-discipline.
So do not be ashamed to testify about our Lord.
~2 Timothy 1:7-8

For the Joy Set Before Me

A woman giving birth to a child has pain because her time has come; but when her baby is born she forgets the anguish because of her joy that a child is born into the world.
John 16:21

While watching a childbirth video, it all came back to me—the pain that was yet to come. Before now, I had shoved thoughts of labor aside to focus on the joy of being pregnant. I didn't want to remember the agony. Watching woman after woman go through labor and delivery, though, vividly reminded me of the pain.

My pre-teen daughters also watched the video. My oldest reached out to hold my hand. They had never seen anything like this before. "The women were in a lot of pain, but as soon as they held their babies, they were full of joy," one daughter commented. The other agreed. Joy? My children saw both the pain and joy of delivery, but they chose to focus on the joy.

John 16:21 tells us that after giving birth the pain is forgotten because of the joy that comes. In essence, that was the theme of the video. In reality, John 16:21 is the theme of every childbirth: forgetting the pain because we are overcome with joy. This is the culmination of childbearing!

Jesus knew this. His disciples understood it and so did my children. None of them had actually experienced the labor or the joy, though, but I had experienced both. Instead of forgetting the anguish because of the joy to come, I was forgetting the joy because of the anguish to come.

Whether this is our first labor or our fifth, we can follow the example of Jesus "who for the joy set before him endured the cross, scorning its shame, and sat down at the right hand of the throne of God" (Hebrews 12:2). The agony which Jesus endured on the cross was far greater than the pain of childbirth. Not only did he experience excruciating, physical pain, but also the torment of God's wrath when He took upon Himself the punishment for our sins.

Look at the symbolism. Our pain in bringing forth new life can be a reminder of the intense suffering of Christ. He hung on the cross to give eternal life for all who believe in Him. What a privilege to be an integral part of God's plan!

While experiencing the pain of labor, we can meditate on Hebrews 12:2 and John 16:21. If we memorize them now, they will be in our hearts when we need them. We can endure the pain to receive the joy set before us.

–MK

Prayer

Jesus, thank You for what You have done for me. I am grateful that my mother endured the pain of childbirth to give me life. Now that I am about to endure pain to give my baby life, help me to focus on the joy set before me. Amen.

For further study ~ John 16 and 17

The Joy Set Before Me

These are the things I fear most about labor:

_____

_____

_____

_____

As I've meditated and worked to memorize John 16:21 and Hebrews 12:2, this is how my perspective has changed:

_____

_____

_____

_____

This is my labor plan to help me deal with the pain so I may focus on the joy set before me:

_____

_____

_____

_____

_____

When anxiety was great within me,
your consolation brought joy to my soul.
~ Psalm 94:19

Preparation

In my Father's house are many rooms; if it were not so,
I would have told you. I am going there to prepare a place for you.

John 14:2

Walk into any baby supply store and you will find a myriad of things for your baby. Some are necessary, some are useful, some are educational and some are merely cute. Even when I'm not pregnant I love these stores. In them there is an excitement, an expectation, an air of preparation. Babies are a new beginning. We buy cribs, and all the bedding to dress them up. We purchase diapers and containers to throw them in. We buy pacifiers to soothe, music to stimulate, books and toys to teach. We want only the best. There are so many things we need and want and so much to choose from.

It's fun to get caught up in the final preparations for the nursery—stitching the finishing touches, hanging the wall decorations, lovingly placing the freshly-laundered clothes in the dresser. All is ready. What joy we experience as we prepare these special places for our babies!

Just as we are preparing a place for our children, God is preparing a special place for us, His children. This place is much greater than we could ever imagine. He has prepared a room, custom designed to bless each person. Only the best will be used and no expense is too great. It will be ready for us on our day of arrival in heaven.

When we sit in our babies' rooms anticipating their arrivals, we can be reminded that God also sits on His throne in heaven anticipating our arrival. Let us be excited that one day we will hear the King of Kings say, "Come, you who are blessed by my Father; take your inheritance, the kingdom prepared for you since the creation of the world" (Matthew 25:34).

–MK

Prayer

Heavenly Father, as I prepare the room for my baby, help me to meditate on the promise You have given. You are preparing a room for me in heaven. The joy and satisfaction I feel about my baby's room are but a small taste of the joy and satisfaction You have towards me as You prepare my heavenly home. Thank You for Your loving care. Amen.

For further study ~ John 14:1-14

Preparation for Me

This is the theme I have chosen to decorate my baby's room:

_____

_____

_____

I have put so much love and care into preparing my baby's room. Here are my thoughts after meditating on God's love and care for me and the room He is preparing in heaven:

_____

_____

_____

_____

How can this heavenly perspective bring joy and comfort to my life?

_____

_____

_____

_____

*However, as it is written:
"No eye has seen, no ear has heard,
no mind has conceived what God has
prepared for those who love him."
~1 Corinthians 2:9*

The Race Set Before Us

Therefore, since we are surrounded by such
a great cloud of witnesses, let us throw off everything
that hinders and the sin that so easily entangles, and let us
run with perseverance the race marked out for us.
Hebrews 12:1

"You can go ahead and go home now," the nurse said.

You've got to be joking. I'm past my due date, my water seems to be leaking, I've made arrangements for my other children to be watched, and I have my suitcase with me. I am not going home! I am ready to have this baby!

I was still mumbling these words as the nurses gently shoved me out of the emergency room and pointed me to the parking garage. I was sullen on the drive home and wanted a nice long soak in a bath of self-pity. I'm huge…I'm swollen…I'm tired of wearing the same old clothes…I'm tired of waiting…I'm tired of trying to be kind when my hormones are raging…I give up.

The Bible compares our lives to a race—a race that is marked out for us. For nine months, we have set before us the stretch of race called pregnancy. It can be a bumpy run, with numerous potholes, and unexpected dips and turns. The end of this stretch can be particularly challenging because of the thick forest that prevents us from seeing what's around the corner.

During the drive home from the hospital that day, I stepped off the race path and my feet got tangled in the weeds of grumbling and self-pity. I could still run with them wrapped around my feet, but my steps would be shaky and my progress slow.

When we find ourselves at a point like this we need to apply Hebrews 12:1 and actively "throw off everything that hinders and the sin that so easily entangles." 1 Corinthians 9:24 says, "Do you not know that in a race all the runners run, but only one gets the prize? Run in such a way as to get the prize."

We have a double blessing awaiting us. As Christians, we will receive a prize from the Father when we finish our race and join Him in heaven. As pregnant ladies, we get a prize when we round the final corner of this stretch. The dense woods will suddenly end as we make the last turn. The sun will burst forth from behind the clouds, and we will see the baby God has created for each of us. Our hearts will leap with joy as our beautiful and precious treasures are placed in our arms. The rest of our journey will never be the same because of the love that we have for our children, and the love our children will give back to us.

–*MLG*

Prayer

Father, You have set the race before me. Please help me to not get entangled as I run. I want to keep before me the prize that is waiting at the end, and the prize that is just around the corner. Amen.

For further study ~ Philippians 2:14-18

The Race Set Before Me

Do I have the mentality of a long distant runner? What can I do to increase my spiritual strength?

_____

_____

_____

Am I allowing anything to distract me from the prizes set before me, both at the end of my pregnancy and the end of my life? If so, what are the distractions?

_____

_____

What should be my motivation for running hard and throwing off everything that hinders me?

_____

_____

_____

_____

You need to persevere so that when
you have done the will of God, you will
receive what he has promised.
~ Hebrews 10:36

Acknowledgments

We would like to thank:

Ken and Rebecca Newbern
>   for generously giving both of us computers which enabled us to work much more efficiently.

Brian Peterson
>   for your guidance and insight.

Marcie Blackwood, Dianne Taulbee, Annisa Carter, Kim Dike, Ann Roberts, Terrie Henderson and Cecilia Kelso
>   for serving our families through this season.

Desiree Pino and Tammy Stoy
>   for your hours and hours of editing.

Richard J. and Mary V. Graham
>   for your faithful encouragement.

The wonderful people of Metro Life Church and Palm Vista Community Church
>   for your prayers, encouragement and tremendous examples of living to glorify God in all that you do.

Our pastors, Danny Jones and Al Pino
>   for your support and commitment to biblical teaching.

Our husbands, Rich Graham and Tim Kelso
>   for serving us heroically in the home, editing our writing and being our best friends through it all.

Our children, Brittany, Becky and Katie Graham; and Emily and Jennalyn Kelso; and the babies in our wombs
>   for giving us more joy than we ever expected and helping us to grow in the fruit of the Spirit.